This book belongs to

....

My TREASURY of FIVE-MINUTE Tales

My TREASURY of FIVE-MINUTE Tales

Forty stories to read and share

p

CONTENTS

Old EVEREST

Everest was one of the biggest horses in the world. He was also one of the strongest. When he was young, and already twice as big as other horses, he pulled the heavy cart filled with peas or potatoes, cabbages or corn, and everything grown on the farm. He took the vegetables from the farm down to the market, and he brought things from the market back to the farm. He pulled the huge machine that cut the wheat to make flour. He pulled the big plough that dug the soil, so the farmer could plant the seed that grew into wheat that made the flour...

...that Everest took to market. He did everything!

Everest was the best...but that was ages ago.

"So why don't you do everything now?" asked Puff the pig.

"The farmer thinks I'm too old," said Everest, sadly. "He is only trying to be kind. He thinks I need a rest."

Jacob the lamb said, "I bet you are still stronger than anything, Everest! Nothing is as strong as you!" The huge horse lowered his head.

"Well...I am not as strong as I was, little one," smiled Everest. "Anyway, farms don't use horses any more. The farmer uses a tractor instead!"

The big old horse had lots of time to think about when he was young and still worked on the farm. He spent most of the time now in his favourite meadow nibbling grass, and, when he grew bored with that, chasing rabbits or chickens, or biting large chunks out of the hedge. But if Parsnip the sheep, Waddle the goose, or Scratchitt the cat were in his field, he would tell them his stories. Sometimes he told the same stories again without realising, but no one really minded.

But Everest still thought about the tractor. It wasn't the tractor's fault. He just wanted to work.

"Can this tractor pull the cart better than you?" asked Parsnip the sheep.

"No," said Everest.

"Can the tractor pull the plough better than you?" asked Waddle the goose.

"No," said Everest.

"Can the tractor cut the wheat better than you?" asked Scratchitt the cat.

"No," said Everest.

"So why did the farmer buy the tractor?" Puff the pig wanted to know. Everest lowered his huge head and sighed.

"He liked the colour," said Everest.

Then one day the farmer said to Everest, "I have a problem with that tractor of mine. It won't start! I would ask you to help, Everest, but I suppose you are enjoying your rest." Everest shook his head from side to side.

"Even so," said the farmer, "I need to plough the field and the plough won't fit a horse, just the tractor! I don't know what to do."

Everest nudged the farmer gently over to the barn where the tractor was kept. His reins and harness were there too. The puzzled farmer picked up an old rope and hooked it on the front of the tractor. Then, as easily as anything, Everest pulled the tractor out. Then he pulled the plough up behind the tractor.

"You mean you can pull both together?" said the farmer. Everest nodded his head up and down. The farmer was amazed! So the farmer hooked the plough to the tractor. Then he hooked the tractor to the horse. And Everest pulled the tractor and the tractor pulled the plough.

Together they ploughed the field in the fastest time ever.

Everest was still the biggest and the strongest... and now the happiest horse in the whole world.

The CHICKLINGS

Duck and Hen both laid some eggs. They were very proud mothers. They would sit with silly smiles on their faces, fondly waiting for their eggs to hatch.

"Duck," said Hen, "let us put the eggs side by side, and see whose eggs are the most beautiful."

"If you like," said Duck, "but I already know mine are."

"Ha!" said Hen. "Wait until you have seen mine!"

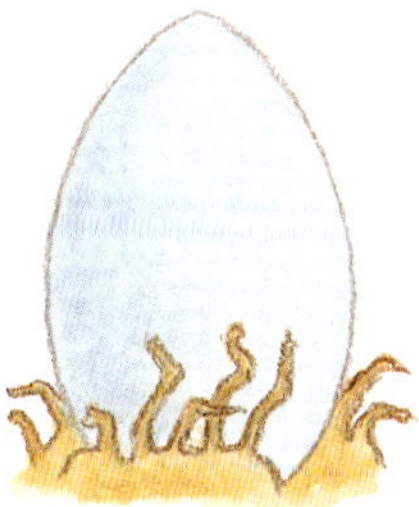

Duck carried her eggs carefully, one by one, to a spot where there was soft hay on the ground. Hen carried her eggs over to the same spot and gently set them down beside Duck's. Duck picked up the first egg from her side.

"Look at this one! This egg is so smooth!" she said. They both looked at how smooth the egg was. Hen picked up an egg too.

"This one is smooth as well...and it is so round! Look at the lovely shape of this egg." They both looked at the shape of the egg. They put back those two eggs and picked up two others.

Duck said, "This one is smooth and shapely, and has beautiful freckles..."

By the time the last one was picked up and put back, the eggs were all mixed up together!

Hen said, "I am fatter than you, so my eggs must be the largest ones." So Duck picked out the smallest eggs and put them back in her nest. Hen picked out the largest eggs and took them back to hers. Then they sat on them until the eggs hatched and out popped fluffy ducklings and chicks.

One day Duck and Hen met with their babies.

"Now!" said Duck proudly. "Aren't these the handsomest ducklings you ever saw?"

"They are quite handsome," replied Hen, "but don't you think these are the most beautiful chicks in the whole world?"

"They are quite beautiful," replied Duck.

The next day, Duck taught her ducklings how to be ducklings.

"Walk behind me, one behind the other!" she told them. "We are going to the pond for swimming lessons." But the ducklings just couldn't walk one behind the other. They ran circles around Duck. They ran over her and under her, until Duck became quite dizzy watching them scoot about. When they reached the pond, the ducklings dipped their feet in the water, shook their heads and refused to go in.

Hen was teaching her chicks how to be chicks. She taught them to scratch and hop backwards to make the worms pop up out of the ground. But the chicks couldn't do it! They fell on their faces instead. She taught them to run all over the farm and look for their own food. They just followed her everywhere in a long line.

When Hen's back was turned, the chicks would cram into the dog's drinking bowl and would not come out! Josh the dog was lying next to his bowl. He opened one eye but didn't seem to mind. He would rather drink from the puddles anyway.

Duck and Hen sighed and sat down together to talk. They knew by now that they had each taken the wrong eggs. The ducklings were chicks, and the chicks were ducklings.

“Never mind,” said Hen. “Let’s just call them chicklings, and we will always be right.”

“One thing we have found out,” said Duck. “is that the chicklings are all beautiful. We would not have mixed them up, otherwise.” Hen agreed, and they sat all afternoon, happily watching their chicklings play.

The ducklings played in the dog’s bowl...

And the chicks played on the dog!

AUNTY and the flowers

Every year on the farm, the animals had a competition. Everyone liked to join in the fun, and there was a prize for the winner. The prize could be for anything. One year, it was for growing the best purple vegetables. Once it was for having the knobbliest knees. (Gladys the duck won that, of course.) Once it was for the animal who could spell 'chrysanthemum'. The prize was not won at all that time…no one in the world can spell chrysanthemum!

This year they decided the

prize would be for the best display of flowers. But who would choose the winner? Most of the animals had already been judges in other years. Some of them had been judges more than once.

If Nelly the hen were the judge, she would make herself the winner. She always did. Bramble the sheep caught her wool on everything. She pulled the tables and chairs down behind her wherever she went.

Blink the pig covered everything in mud.

Rambo the big horse couldn't even get into the tent!

But Aunty the goat wanted the job. She told the others how much she liked flowers. So why not? Aunty had never been a judge before and so she was chosen.

The big day came. Everyone had been busy for days. The tent was full of flowers, full of colour and light. There were no brown leaves on the flowers. There were no creepy-crawlies on the leaves. There was just a lovely smell of roses, and the animals waiting excitedly for the doors to open. Perfect!

The judge, Aunty the goat, went first. She looked very important. Then all the rest came in, one at a time. Last was Rambo, the big horse, who just poked in his head. Aunty was taken to the first display by Bramble the sheep.

"So I just choose which flowers I like best?" Aunty asked.

"Yes, we walk along the table, and whichever display you think is best wins the prize. This is Blink's display. She has spent all morning getting it just right."

"It's called 'Daisies and Dandelions'," said Blink proudly. The flowers were white and yellow and looked very pretty in a bright blue mug. Aunty looked at them carefully. She sniffed them. And then she ate them.

The others were so surprised, that they couldn't speak! They just stared as Aunty went to the next one, 'Buttercups and Roses'. She ate them too!

The goat tilted her head back, half closed her eyes in a very thoughtful sort of way, and compared 'Buttercups and Roses' with 'Daisies and Dandelions'.

Moving along the line, she ate 'Cowslips and Honeysuckle'. Then she ate 'Poppies and Krezanthasums... Crissansathums... Chrismasathumbs... Poppies and another flower we can't spell!' Aunty wrinkled up her nose.

"Bit sour, that," she said. She turned at last and saw all the others looking at her with their mouths open. She looked from one to the other, red poppies drooping from the sides of her mouth.

"What?" she said, puzzled. "What!"

Rambo said gently, "You were supposed to judge how pretty the flowers are!"

Aunty was amazed.

"Flowers are pretty as well?" she asked.

Everyone burst out laughing. They had to explain it all to Aunty. She thought the whole idea of just looking at flowers was very odd.

There was no time to pick more flowers and start again. Instead, they gave Blink the prize…Aunty had decided that Blink's 'Daisies and Dandelions' tasted the best!

At the end, the judge is always given a bunch of flowers as a small, 'thank you' gift. Aunty was so pleased…she ate it!

Cuddly's JUMPER

Cuddly Sheep and Stout Pig were going to show the others how to knit. Cuddly Sheep was really good at knitting. But she needed her friend, Stout Pig, to help with the wool. Stout Pig couldn't knit, not even a little bit, but he was very good at spinning the wool for Cuddly to use.

Wool has to be made into yarn before you can knit with it. Yarn is made by twisting it, like string.

That is what Stout did. He collected all the loose bits of wool that caught on thorny bushes around the farm and made long, beautiful lengths of yarn out of them. Then

Cuddly used Stout Pig's yarn to knit lots of pretty things. She could knit woolly socks. She could knit woolly hats. She could knit the best woolly jumpers in the world!

Cuddly and Stout sat close to each other. Stout Pig sat with his back against a low hedge and Cuddly sat on the other side. The pig pulled out lengths of wool from a pile under the hedge. He started to spin the wool on his wheel, until it was twisted into yarn and long enough to knit. Then he gave the end to Cuddly.

Cuddly made little loops of the wool and put them on two fat knitting needles. Then she started knitting.

"Knit one, purl one, knit two together," she whispered to herself. Only knitters know what these secret words mean. They must be magic words, because they are whispered over and over again.

"Knit one, purl one, knit two together."

The jumper quickly started to take shape. As it grew in size, the animals watching could see it was nearly all white, just like the colour of Cuddly's own

woolly jumper, with little bits in purple, like the berries on the hedge.

"Knit one, purl one, knit two together."

Stout had to work hard on the other side of the hedge to keep up with Cuddly Sheep.

"Knit one, purl one, knit two together..."

Cuddly looked up. "Is it getting late? I'm getting a bit cold," she said. None of the others felt cold.

"You can put my blanket on," said Pebbles the horse. He pulled his blanket over Cuddly's shoulders. But Cuddly got colder. And colder!

"I keep warm in the straw," said Saffron the cow. She covered Cuddly with straw. But the more Cuddly

knitted, the colder she got. And the hotter Stout became.

Cuddly was trying to finish the jumper quickly before she froze. The faster she knitted, the faster Stout Pig had to turn the spinning wheel, and he was soon in a sweat!

Then the jumper was finished...and Cuddly was shivering! Her teeth were chattering! Stout Pig flopped over the spinning wheel, trying to get his breath back. He was so hot and tired. Pebbles looked hard at Stout.

"Where did the wool come from that you were spinning?" he asked.

"I used that bundle of wool under the hedge," said Stout. "It was here when I came."

Pebbles' large head followed the wool from the spinning wheel over the hedge. There was only Cuddly there. "Cuddly," said Pebbles '…I think you have been knitting your own wool!"

Cuddly jumped up in surprise. The blanket and the straw fell off. She was bare all around her middle. No wonder she was cold. Her wool was all gone!

"Oh well," said Cuddly Sheep, taking out the needles from her knitting. "Never mind! I have a nice thick new jumper to keep me warm!"

Clever BOOGIE

Boogie was a very clever pig. Most pigs aren't clever. They can't do sums. They can't tie their own shoelaces. Every single day they are given pig food to eat, and they say, "Oink! Oink! Pig food! My favourite!" They don't remember it's always the same.

But Boogie remembered every horrible meal he'd ever had, and was really fed up with pig food. It tasted like minced rubbish! Boogie lived in his own pen. It had a little shelter to keep the rain off, and a small run to play in. In the field outside the pigpen lived a sheep, a horse and a cow. There were trees in the field too, but none near Boogie.

One day, acorns started falling from the biggest tree. The tree was a long way from Boogie, but just a few acorns bounced over and into his pen. Apples began falling from another tree, and one rolled and rolled, until it rolled into Boogie's pen.

Now, usually the only thing inside a pigpen is a pig. They eat everything else! They eat the grass, the roots, worms, stinging nettles, everything! All that is left is a pig in mud! Pigs think anything else in a pen must be food. So Boogie ate the acorns.

You probably know that acorns are really horrible to eat, but Boogie thought they were delicious! Then he ate the apple. He had never eaten anything so good in his life! He wanted all the acorns and apples! They were all around him, but he could not reach them. But he was a clever pig after all. Suddenly he had an idea.

Next to Boogie's pigpen was an old animal shed that had fallen to bits. Bricks and wood were spread about and wavy metal roof panels lay nearby.

Boogie said to the cow, "Will you move that metal roof for me? I'll give you some of my food if you do."

"I have all this grass to eat!" said the cow.

"But that's just plain grass," said Boogie. "This is pig food flavour in lumps!"

"Oh, all right!" said the cow. She pushed the roof under the apple tree.

"There! Is that in the right place?"

"Just move it forward...now turn it towards me... Good!"

Boogie gave the cow some of his pig food. The cow chewed for ages before she realised pig food did not have any actual taste in it. She spat it out.

"Pwah! Tastes like minced rubbish!" she said, and trotted off.

Boogie said to the horse, "Will you move that barrel for me? I'll give you some of my food if you do."

"I have all this grass to eat!" said the horse.

"But yours is green grass," said Boogie. "This is rich brown pig food in lumps!" So the horse moved the barrel where Boogie wanted it and was given the rest of the pig food.

"Yuck!" said the horse, when he tried it. "Do you really eat this rubbish?" And he galloped off too.

Boogie looked at the sheep. The sheep said, "I know – you want me to move something! I'll do it, but please don't give me any pig food!"

The sheep moved the drainpipe to where Boogie wanted it.

When the next apple fell, it rolled down the iron roof into the drainpipe and flew into Boogie's pen!

An acorn bounced off the barrel, and soon there were apples and acorns falling everywhere and bouncing into Boogie's pen.

Boogie dashed around, catching apples and acorns before they could even touch the ground!

And he never had to eat pig food again!

– Desmond – GROWS UP

Desmond was the smallest monkey in the group. He couldn't wait to grow up.

"Will you measure me?" Desmond asked his best friend Rodney.

"I only measured you last Monday, and now it's Friday," said Rodney. "You won't have grown in four days!"

"I have," said Desmond stubbornly. "My bones have grown...you'll see."

Rodney took him to the tallest tree in the jungle and made him stand with his back against it. Then he made a mark on the trunk at the top of Desmond's head. It was in the same place as the last mark.

"See," he said, "you are still the same size."

"Botheration!" said Desmond.

One thing Desmond really wanted to do was collect coconuts. All the big monkeys collected coconuts. The small monkeys had to do the washing up! It wasn't fair.

Later he spoke to his friend Bubbles.

"Watch the top of my head," he said to her.

"Whatever for, Dethmond?" said Bubbles. She always called him Dethmond.

"Just watch," said Desmond.

So Bubbles watched the top of his head.

"Well?" asked Desmond.

"Well what?" replied Bubbles.

"Am I growing? Can you see me growing?"

"No, of course not!" she said.

"I knew it!" said Desmond. "I knew it! I'm never going to grow."

"Dethmond," said Bubbles, "you say this every single day. You will grow! Honestly you will."

But Desmond was not so sure.

"What can I do to get taller?" he asked Rodney.

"Wait!" said Rodney. So Desmond stood next to Rodney...and waited.

And waited ...and waited...and waited!

"You won't grow that fast!" laughed Rodney. He looked down at his friend. "It will be ages before you grow up."

But Desmond didn't have ages. He wanted to collect coconuts...NOW! He tried to stretch. He asked all his friends to pull on his arms and legs. He asked them to squeeze him so that he would get thinner and taller. He hung from the branches of trees by his toes. But nothing worked!

Every day he watched the other monkeys climb the tall palm trees. Every day he watched as they picked the coconuts and dropped them to the ground.

One day there was a competition to see who could collect the most coconuts. Rodney was the favourite to win. He climbed to the top and wriggled through the palm leaves, and then...oh dear...he got stuck! He made a face as only monkeys can!

"Help!" he called,"I can't move."

One of the other big monkeys went up to try and help, but he was too big to get through the leaves.

"Let me try," begged Desmond.

"If you like," they said grudgingly.

Desmond hurtled up the trunk. At the top he was small enough to reach his friend and help him to get free. Then he picked six or seven coconuts and dropped them to the ground.

When they climbed down the other monkeys crowded round to pat Desmond on the back.

Desmond was as proud as could be.

“Wow!” said Bubbles. “No one has ever, ever climbed a tree that fast before.”

“Maybe you are all too big!” said Desmond happily. “Perhaps I won’t be in such a hurry to grow up after all!”

After that he didn’t worry so much about being small, especially after he collected more coconuts than anyone else, and won the competition!

The Smiley CROCODILE

Open-wide was the friendliest crocodile for miles around. While all the grumpy crocodiles were snapping and snarling and being very cross, Open-wide grinned at everyone. He had a very, very big smile.

"You smile too much," the others told him.

"Be fierce...like a real crocodile!"

"I'll try," said Open-wide, and he put on a scowly face.

It lasted two seconds and then the smile came back again.

"How was that?" he asked.

"Hopeless!" the others said. It was no good, he couldn't be grumpy if he tried.

One day, some hippos came to the river. They were very large and there were a lot of them. They waded into the part of the river that the crocodiles liked the best. They splashed and shouted, they dipped and dived, they made a lot of waves and a lot of noise. They were having a really good time.

Open-wide liked watching them having fun. He liked it when they sank to the bottom and then came up very slowly making lots of ripples. He liked it

when they had a contest to see who could make the biggest splash. He liked it when they blew fountains of water up into the air. The grumpy crocodiles didn't like it one little bit!

"We'll soon get rid of them," they said.

Open-wide saw a baby hippo playing in the water. His name was Sausage.

"I bet you can't do this!" said Sausage to Open-wide, and he blew a million bubbles so that they floated in a cloud across the top of the water.

"I bet I can," said Open-wide. And he did... through his nose!

"What about this?" said Sausage, and he turned on his back and sank below the surface. Open wide did the same, and then he swam very fast to the opposite bank of the river. They played like this all day...and every day after that! Open-wide had never had such a good time.

The grumpy crocodiles were very fed up. They got together to think of ways of getting rid of the hippos. First they tried to look fierce by showing lots of teeth. The hippos just smiled...and showed even bigger teeth!

Then the grumpy crocodiles tried being rude. "Scram!" they shouted...and when that didn't work, "Smelly old hippos!" The hippos thought it was a joke.

Next they charged the hippos while they were swimming. The hippos calmly sank to the bottom of the river where it was too deep for the crocodiles.

The crocodiles didn't know what else to do.

Open-wide had an idea!

"Why don't I just smile at them and ask them nicely if they will move?" he said.

"Pooh!" said the crocodiles. "Fat lot of good that will do!"

Open-wide didn't give up. "Please?"

"Oh, go on then," said the grumpy crocodiles,

"but it won't work, you'll see."

But it did! The hippos liked Open-wide. He had a big smile just like them. They listened politely when he explained that the crocodiles didn't really like fun. They would rather be on their own and grumpy.

"We'll move further down the river if you will still come and play with Sausage," they said.

And that's what happened. The crocodiles were amazed! They didn't say anything to Open-wide, but secretly they wondered if smiling *was* better than scowling after all!

Leo Makes A FRIEND

Leo was quite a shy lion. His mum and dad and brothers and sisters were all much bolder. Sometimes he was sad because he didn't have any friends of his own.

"Mum," he said one day, "why will no one play with me?"

"Because other animals think you're frightening," said Mum.

"Pooh," said Leo, "why would anyone be frightened of me?"

"Because you're a lion," said Mum.

It was a lovely day. Leo felt sure he would make a new friend today.

He came to some trees where a group of small monkeys were playing. When the monkeys saw Leo they scampered to the top of the tallest trees.

"Hello," called out Leo.

There was no answer. He could see lots of eyes staring down at him.

"Hello," he called again. "Won't you come down and play with me?"

There was silence. Then one of the monkeys blew a loud raspberry.

"Go away," he said rudely, "we don't like lions!"

"Why not?" asked Leo, giving him a big smile.

"Your teeth are too big," said the monkey, and giggled noisily.

Leo walked on until he came to a deep pool where a hippopotamus and her baby were bathing. Leo watched them playing in the water.

"Hi!" called out Leo. "Can I come in the water with you?"

"No!" said Mummy Hippo.

"But I'd like to play," said Leo.

"So would I!" said Baby Hippo.

"No, you wouldn't," said Mummy Hippo firmly. "You don't play with lions."

"Why not?" asked Baby.

"Because they might eat you!" said Mummy.

"Oh dear," said Baby Hippo.

Puzzled, Leo walked on. He came to an ostrich with its head buried in the sand.

"What are you doing?" asked Leo in surprise.

"Hiding from you!" said the ostrich gruffly.

"But I can still see you!" said Leo.

"But I can't see you!" said the ostrich.

Leo stuck his head in the sand. It felt awful. Sand got in his eyes and in his mouth.

"It feels horrible," he said, spitting sand everywhere.

"Come and play with me instead," said Leo.

"Not likely," said the ostrich. "I don't play with lions, they roar!"

Leo walked on. He saw a snake sunbathing on a rock. He touched the snake gently with his paw.

"Play with me," he said.

"Ouch!" said the snake. "Your claws are too sharp."

Feeling very fed up, Leo sat down under a tree to eat his picnic.

He was all alone. There was no one else in sight.

"I shall just have to get used to playing by myself," he thought.

Suddenly, he heard a small voice say, "Hello!"

Leo looked round. He could see a pair of yellow eyes peeping at him from behind a tree.

"You won't want to play with me," said Leo grumpily, "I've got a loud roar!"

"So have I," said the voice.

"And I've got sharp claws," said Leo.

"So have I," said the voice again.

"And big teeth," said Leo.

"I've got big teeth, too," said the voice.

"What are you?" asked Leo, interested now.

"I'm a lion, of course!"

And into the clearing walked another little lion.

"I'm a lion, too," said Leo, grinning. "Would you like to share my picnic?"

"Yes, please!" said the other lion. They ate the picnic and played for the rest of the afternoon.

"I like being a lion," said Leo happily. He had made a friend at last!

Grandma Elephant's Birthday

"Boris," said his parents, "it's a special day today. Can you remember why?" They say elephants never forget, but Boris never *remembered.* He wrinkled his forehead and thought very hard.

"Do I start school today?" he said.

"No," said Dad, shaking his head.

"Is it my birthday?" asked Boris.

"Getting closer," said Mum. "It's Grandma Elephant's birthday! I want you to take her this basket of fruit. Can you remember where she lives?"

"Yes," nodded Boris. Mum gave him the basket of fruit and watched him leave.

Boris walked through the forest. It was very quiet and shady.

"Boo!" shouted a voice suddenly. Boris looked round and saw a very strange animal. It looked like a mouse with wings.

"Do I know you?" asked Boris

"I'm Fruit Bat, ninny," said the fruit bat.

"What do fruit bats do?" asked Boris.

"Eat fruit, of course," said Fruit Bat. "Where are you off to?"

"It's Grandma Elephant's birthday, but I can't remember how to get to her house," said Boris.

"If I tell you, will you give me some fruit?" asked the bat.

Boris nodded.

"That's the path over there," pointed the bat. And he took an apple from Boris's basket.

The path was very narrow. Right in the middle, blocking the way, was a huge gorilla.

"Where do you think you're going?" asked Gorilla.

"I'm taking this basket of fruit to Grandma," said Boris bravely. "It's her birthday."

"Don't you remember who I am?" asked Gorilla.

"Err...you're Crocodile," said Boris.

"No," said Gorilla. "Try again!"

"You're Rhinoceros," Boris tried again.

"If you can't remember who I am," said Gorilla, "you'll have to pay a forfeit."

"What's a forfeit?" Boris asked.

"Something you give me if you get the wrong answer!" said Gorilla. Boris couldn't remember so Gorilla took two bananas and let Boris pass.

Reaching a crossroads, Boris didn't know which path to take.

"Take the left path," said a voice high above him.

Looking up, Boris saw Giraffe with his head sticking out of the top of a tree.

"How can you be sure?" asked Boris.

"Are you going to Grandma Elephant's?" asked Giraffe.

"Yes," said Boris.

"I can see her house from up here," said Giraffe.

"Thank you," said Boris. "Have some fruit!"

"That's very kind of you," said Giraffe. He lowered his head and took a pear from the basket.

When Boris arrived at Grandma's house, all that was left in the basket was one juicy plum! What would Grandma say? Would she be cross? He needn't have worried. Grandma hugged him and took him into the kitchen.

There, sitting round the table, were Fruit Bat, Gorilla and Giraffe, all wearing party hats.

In the middle of the table was a big birthday cake, a large

wobbly red jelly, and *all* the fruit they had taken from Boris's basket.

"How sweet of you to arrange a surprise party for me, Boris," said Grandma, hugging him again. They had a lovely time. They played 'Pass the Parcel'. They played 'Hunt the Thimble'. They sang 'Happy Birthday Grandma Elephant'. Grandma said it was the nicest birthday she could remember.

Boris couldn't even remember the way home. So when the party was over his friends took him all the way back. Mum was so pleased to see him.

"Aren't you going to introduce me to your friends?" she asked.

"This is Bat Fruit, Crocodile and Giraffe," said Boris.

Everybody laughed. Silly Boris...what a memory!

COPYCAT
— MAX —

Max was a little tiger with a bad habit. He was a terrible copycat! He copied everyone and everything. When the parrot said, "Pretty Polly, Pretty Polly!" Max repeated it. "Pretty Polly, Pretty Polly!" Then, when the parrot got cross and said, "Shut up, Max, shut up Max," he repeated that as well. It was very annoying.

One day, he set off to explore.

"I shall copy everything I see," he said to himself. And that's when the trouble really started!

First, he saw a bat hanging upside down on the branch of a tree. It was trying to get to sleep.

"I shall go to sleep like that, too," said Max.

"You can't," said the bat. "Only bats sleep like this."

"Hmmm!" said Max, thoughtfully. And he climbed up to the nearest branch, hooked his feet over it and hung upside down.

"Goodnight," he said and shut his eyes.

The next thing he knew he had landed with a crash on the ground.

"I told you!" said the bat. Max picked himself up.

Next, he met a stork standing on one leg.

"Why are you doing that?" asked Max.

"Because it's comfortable," said the stork.

"How long can you do it for?" asked Max.

"For ages!" said the stork. "Only birds can stand like this."

"Hmmm!" said Max, and lifted up one leg.

"Now lift up two more," said the stork. Max did, and fell in a heap on the ground.

"Told you!" said the stork. Max picked himself up.

Exploring further, he met a brown chameleon sitting on a green leaf. The amazing thing about chameleons is that they can change colour

when they want to. The chameleon saw Max and changed his colour to green, like the leaf! Max could no longer see him.

"Where have you gone?" asked Max, looking everywhere.

"I'm still here," said the chameleon. "Watch this," he added, and he jumped onto a red flower and turned...red!

"Watch this then," said Max, and he lay down on some grass. "Now I'm green," he said.

"No, you're not," said the chameleon. "Only chameleons can change colour."

"Hmmm!" said Max. He rolled over and over in some mud.

"Look," he said, "now I'm brown." Then he rolled in some white feathers. The feathers stuck to the mud.

"Look," he said, "now I'm all white!"

"It won't last," said the chameleon.

Max decided to set off for home. He passed the stork still standing on one leg. The stork didn't recognize him. He passed the bat, still hanging upside down. The bat didn't recognize him.

He arrived home late in the evening. His brothers and sisters were playing down by the river. They saw a white figure coming towards them.

"WOOooo!" wailed Max, pretending to be a ghost. "I've come to get you!" The tiger cubs were so scared, they rushed into the river and started to swim to the other side.

"WOOooo!" wailed Max and rushed in after them. Of course, as soon as Max got wet, the mud and feathers disappeared. When the others saw it was only Max they were really cross.

"You frightened us," they told him.

"It was only a joke," said Max.

They only agreed to forgive him if he promised not to copy anything again.

"Oh, all right," said Max. And for the moment, he meant it!

– A Perfect – PUPPY

Polly had wanted a puppy for a long time, so when Mummy and Daddy said yes, she couldn't wait to get to the pet shop.

At the pet shop, Polly inspected the puppies one by one. She wanted to be sure that she chose the right one. After all, her puppy had to be perfect.

“That one’s too big,” said Polly, pointing to a Great Dane. “And that one’s too small.” She pointed to a tiny Chihuahua.

“How about this one?” said Mummy, stroking an Afghan hound.

“Too hairy.”

“Well, how about this boxer?” said Daddy, tickling its pink tummy.

“Not hairy enough.”

“This one’s nice,” said the shopkeeper, patting a poodle.

"Too curly," Polly declared.

Another puppy was too noisy. And two more were too quiet. Before long, there weren't many puppies left. Polly was about to give up, when something soft rubbed against her leg.

"Ah, perfect," she cried, picking up a small bundle of black and white fur.

"Err, what kind of puppy is it?" asked Daddy.

"It's my puppy," sighed Polly.

"It's a mongrel," said the shopkeeper. "I think it's part spaniel and part collie. We're not really sure."

"I don't care what he is," smiled Polly. "He's just perfect. I'm going to call him Danny."

Danny whined as he left the pet shop. And he whined all the way home. But he stopped whining when he saw the cat. Then he started barking instead.

"He'll be okay once he gets used to us," said Mummy. Polly hoped she was right.

In the afternoon, they took Danny for a walk in the park. Polly took some bread to feed to the ducks. But as soon as Danny saw the ducks he started to bark. Then he began to chase them. He didn't stop until the last duck had flown away.

Polly was so upset that Daddy bought her an ice-cream to cheer her up.

"He's just a puppy. He's got a lot to learn," explained Daddy. But Polly wasn't listening. Danny had jumped up and stolen her ice-cream. Polly was beginning to wonder if she'd chosen the right puppy.

When they got home, Polly decided to show Danny her toys. She was introducing all her dolls and cuddly toys, when Danny pounced on her favourite teddy.

"He's got Mr Fluffy," cried Polly, as Danny raced from the room into the garden. When he came back, Mr Fluffy was gone.

Polly was furious. She waved an angry finger at Danny. "You're not a perfect puppy," she said. "I don't think you'll ever learn."

Poor Danny, he hung his head and slunk away under the table and wouldn't come out all evening.

The next morning, Polly was woken up by something wet pressed against her cheek. She opened her eyes to see what it was. It was Danny, wagging his tail. And in his mouth was Mr Fluffy! Danny dropped Mr Fluffy on the floor for Polly to pick up.

"Good boy, Danny," laughed Polly, tickling his ears. "You are a perfect puppy, after all!"

– Monty the – MONGREL

Monty was a very curious puppy. He liked nothing better than exploring the garden.

"Don't go far," Mummy would say. But Monty wasn't worried about getting lost. He was a very good explorer.

One day, a big lorry pulled up outside the house where Monty lived. Two men began carrying things out of the house. One of them said something about moving, but Monty was just a puppy and didn't know what that meant.

One of the men left the gate open so, when no one was looking, Monty crept out.

Monty had a wonderful time sniffing around other people's gardens. He found lots of yummy things to eat. And some really lovely things to roll in.

After a while, Monty began to feel tired. He was such a good explorer that he sniffed his way home without any trouble.

But when he got there, he couldn't believe his eyes. Everyone, including Mummy and all his brothers and sisters, had gone.

Monty was very surprised but he wasn't too worried. After all, he was a very good explorer. He began sniffing at once.

He soon found himself in the park where he met a group of dogs.

"Who are you?" asked one.

"What kind of dog are you?" asked another.

Monty didn't know who to answer first, so he just stopped sniffing and stared.

"Well, he's not a Poodle," sniffed the first dog, who Monty couldn't help thinking looked like a ball of cotton wool. "He's far too rough."

"He's definitely not a dachshund," said another dog. Monty tried hard not to laugh. He'd never seen anything so long.

"He's certainly not an Old English sheepdog," barked a third dog. "He's just not hairy enough."

"Hmm!" grunted a fourth dog, who had the flattest nose Monty had ever seen. He walked around Monty and stared at him from all sides. Then he stopped and shuddered. "I don't think he's a special kind of dog. I think he's a MONGREL."

"Yes!" barked Monty. He liked the sound of that.

"Well if that's the case," sniffed the cotton wool dog, "he'd better hang out with Tinker."

The long dog nudged Monty towards Tinker. Monty thought Tinker was the most handsome dog he'd ever seen. He had short legs, long ears and a wonderful curly tail. He also had kind eyes.

"Take no notice of them," said Tinker. "They're just trying to help."

Monty gave Tinker a lick, and before long he was telling Tinker about his family.

"Let's walk around the park," said Tinker. "If we follow our noses, we might find your family."

In the park, Monty sniffed the air. He could smell a very familiar smell. Then, he heard a very familiar bark. Suddenly, a huge brown dog bounded out of one of the houses on the other side of the park.

"Run for your lives," yelped thc cotton wool dog.

"Help! It's a giant," barked the flat-nosed dog.

"Mummy!" shouted Monty.

"Monty!" barked Mummy. "Thank goodness you're safe."

"Tinker looked after me," said Monty happily.

"So you're a Great Dane puppy," laughed Tinker. "Not a mongrel, after all."

Milly the GREEDY —Puppy—

Milly the Labrador puppy just loved eating. She wasn't fussy what she ate, and didn't really mind whom it belonged to.

"You'll get fat," warned Tom, the farm cat. But Milly was too busy chewing a tasty fishbone to take any notice.

One day, Milly was in a particularly greedy mood. Before breakfast she sneaked into the kitchen and ate Tom's biscuits. After a big breakfast of fresh sardines and milk, she took a short break before nibbling her way through the horse's oats. The horse didn't seem to mind.

Then Milly had a quick nap. She felt quite hungry when she woke up, so she ate all the tastiest titbits from the pig's trough. But she made sure she left plenty of room for lunch.

After a light lunch, Milly couldn't help feeling just a bit hungry – so she wolfed down Farmer Jones's meat pie. He'd left it on the window ledge so he obviously didn't want it.

After that, Milly knocked over the dustbin and rifled through the kitchen waste. It was full of the yummiest leftovers. You really wouldn't believe the things that people throw away.

There was just enough time for another nap before nipping into the milking shed for milking

time. Milly always enjoyed lapping up the odd bucketful of fresh milk when Farmer Jones wasn't looking.

Dinner was Milly's favourite meal of the day. It was amazing how fast she could eat a huge bowl of meat and biscuits.

Before going to bed, Milly walked around the yard cleaning up the scraps the hens had left behind. Wasn't she a helpful puppy!

Just as Milly was chewing a particularly tasty bit of bread, she saw something black out of the corner of her eye. It was Tom the farm cat, out for his evening stroll. If there was one thing Milly liked doing best of all, it was eating Tom's dinner when he wasn't looking.

Milly raced across the yard, around the barn and through the cat flap.

"Woof! Woof!" yelped Milly. She was stuck half-way through the cat flap. Greedy Milly had eaten so much food that her tummy was too big to fit through.

"Ha! Ha!" laughed the farm animals, who thought it served Milly right for eating all their food.

"Oh, dear!" smiled Tom when he came back to see what all the noise was about. He caught hold of Milly's legs and tried pulling her out. Then he tried pushing her out. But it was no good, she was stuck.

All the farm animals joined in. They pulled and pulled, until, POP! Out flew Milly.

Poor Milly felt so silly that she never ate anyone else's food again – unless they offered, that is!

Hooray for PEPPER!

Pepper was a very noisy puppy. He wasn't a bad puppy. He was just so happy that he barked all day long.

"Woof! Woof!" he barked at the cat, and she hissed and ran away.

"Woof! Woof!" he barked at the birds, and they flew up into the tree.

"Woof! Woof!" he barked at the tree, and it waved its branches angrily.

"Woof! Woof!" he barked

at the postman, and he hurried down the garden path.

"Quiet, Pepper!" shouted Jimmy, Pepper's owner. But Pepper just barked back cheerfully.

One day, Pepper had been barking so much that everyone was trying very hard to ignore him.

"Be quiet, Pepper," said Jimmy, as he lay down on the lawn. "I'm going to read my book and I can't concentrate if you keep barking."

Pepper tried his very best not to bark. He tried not to watch the butterflies and bees flitting about the garden. He tried to ignore the bright yellow ball lying on the path. And he tried extra hard not to bark at the birds flying high up in the sky. But everywhere he looked, there were things to bark at, so he decided to stare at the blades of grass on the lawn instead.

As he stared at the grass, Pepper was sure that it began to move. And as he carried on staring, Pepper was sure he could hear a strange slithering sound. He was just about to bark when he remembered Jimmy's words. He carried on staring. Now he could hear a hissing sound. Pepper stared more closely at the grass.

Pepper suddenly started to bark wildly.

"Woof! Woof!" he barked at the grass.

"Sshhh!" groaned Jimmy, as he turned the page of his book.

But Pepper didn't stop. He had spotted something long and slippery slithering across the lawn – something with a long tongue that hissed. Pepper didn't know what it was. But he did know that it didn't look very friendly, and it was heading straight for Jimmy.

"Woof! Woof! WOOF!" barked Pepper, starting to panic. Wasn't anyone going to take any notice of him?

"Quiet, Pepper!" called Jimmy's dad from the house. "How many times have I told you to stop barking?"

But Pepper did not stop barking. He simply barked louder still. Jimmy sat up, and looked around. It wasn't like Pepper to bark quite so much.

"Snake!" yelled Jimmy, pointing at the long slippery snake coming towards him.

Pepper carried on barking as Jimmy's dad raced across the lawn and scooped Jimmy up in his arms. And he carried on barking until a man from the animal rescue centre arrived to take away the snake.

Later, after the man from the animal rescue centre had taken the snake away, Jimmy patted Pepper and gave him an extra-special doggy treat.

"Hooray for Pepper!" laughed Jimmy. "Your barking really saved the day." That night, Pepper was even allowed to sleep on Jimmy's bed.

And from that day on, Pepper decided that it was best if he kept his bark for special occasions!

CUDDLES to the Rescue

Cuddles was a very smart little poodle. Her hair was snowy white and fell in perfect curls. Her claws were always neatly trimmed and polished. She wore a crisp red bow on top of her head. And she never, ever went out without her sparkly dog collar.

Once a week Cuddles was sent to the Poodle Parlour, where she was given a wash, cut and blow dry. And every morning her owner, Gilly, brushed and styled Cuddles' hair until they both looked exactly the same!

But although Cuddles was the smartest, most pampered pooch around, she was not happy. You see, she didn't have any doggy friends.

Whenever Gilly took her walking in the park, Cuddles tried her best to make friends but the other dogs didn't want to know her.

"Here comes Miss Snooty," they would bark. Then they'd point and snigger, before racing away to have some playful puppy fun.

And Cuddles was never let off her velvet lead. "Those other dogs look rough," explained Gilly. "You're far safer walking with me."

Cuddles would have loved to run around with the other dogs. She thought that chasing sticks and balls looked like brilliant fun. And she was sure that she'd be able to swim in the lake if only Gilly would let her.

But the other dogs didn't know that Cuddles wanted to be one of them. They just took one look at her snowy white curls and sparkly collar and thought that she was too posh for them.

"She doesn't want to get her paws dirty," Mrs Collie explained to Skip, her youngest pup, when he asked why Cuddles was always on a lead.

Then one day, Cuddles was walking with Gilly in the park, when she saw Skip chasing ducks beside the lake.

Cuddles looked around but Mrs Collie was nowhere to be seen.

"Be careful!" barked Cuddles, as Skip bounced up and down with excitement

But Skip was far too busy to listen. Then, as a duck took off, Skip took an extra large bounce, and threw himself into the lake.

"Stop!" barked Cuddles. But it was no good, Skip was already up to his chin in water.

"Help! Help!" barked Skip, as he splashed about wildly in the lake.

Cuddles looked around, but no one else had noticed the little pup in the water. She gave a loud bark, and then, using all her strength, pulled the lead from Gilly's hand.

"Cuddles!" cried Gilly. But Cuddles was already in the water. Gilly looked on in horror as Cuddles caught the struggling pup by the scruff of his neck and dragged him ashore.

Once on dry land, Cuddles gave herself a big shake, then started to lick Skip dry.

"Cuddles," breathed Skip, who was quickly recovering from his ordeal.

"Cuddles!" cried Gilly, pointing in horror at her soaking wet curls and muddy paws.

"Will you play with me?" barked Skip, wagging his tail hopefully.

Cuddles looked at Gilly, then at Skip. Surely Gilly wouldn't mind just this once.

Gilly looked in amazement as Cuddles raced Skip across the park to find Mrs Collie. She had never seen Cuddles look so scruffy. But, much more importantly, she had never seen her look so happy.

After that, Gilly always let Cuddles play with the other dogs in the park. But she always made sure that she had an extra big wash and brush when she got home. But Cuddles didn't mind. She had so many doggy friends that she was the happiest little poodle around.

The NAUGHTY — Kitten —

Ginger was a naughty little kitten. He didn't always mean to be naughty, but somehow things just turned out that way.

"You really should be more careful," warned Mummy. But Ginger was too busy getting into trouble to listen.

One day, Ginger was in a particularly playful mood. First, he tried to play tag with his smallest sister – and chased her right up an old apple tree. It took Daddy all morning to get her down.

Then, Ginger dropped cream all over the dog's tail. The dog whirled round and round as he tried to lick it off. He got so dizzy that he fell right over. That really made Ginger laugh until his sides hurt.

After that, Ginger thought it would be fun to play hide-and-seek with the mice. He frightened them so much that they refused to come out of their hole for the rest of the day.

Then, Ginger crept up behind the rabbit and shouted, "HI!" The poor rabbit was so surprised that he fell head-first into his breakfast. Ginger thought he looked ever so funny covered in lettuce leaves. The rabbit was very cross.

For his next trick, Ginger knocked over a wheelbarrow full of apples while he was trying to fly like a bird. He really couldn't help laughing when the apples knocked his little brother flying into the air.

And when one of the

apples splashed into the garden pond, Ginger decided to go apple bobbing. How he laughed as the goldfish bumped into each other in their hurry to get out of his way.

Ginger laughed so much that, WHO-OO-AH! he began to lose his balance. He stopped laughing as he tried to stop himself falling into the pond. But, SPLASH! it was no good – he fell right in.

"Help! I can't swim," wailed Ginger, splashing wildly around. But he needn't have worried, the water only reached up to his knees. "Yuck!" he moaned, squirting out a mouthful of water.

"Ha, ha, ha!" laughed the other kittens, who had come to see what the noise was about. And the dog and the rabbit soon joined in.

"You really should be more careful," said Mummy, trying not to smile.

"It's not funny," said Ginger. He gave the other animals a hard glare as Daddy pulled him out of the pond. But then he caught sight of his reflection in the water. He did look very funny. Soon he was laughing as loud as the others.

After that, Ginger tried hard not to be quite so naughty. And do you know what? He even succeeded ...some of the time!

— Where's — WANDA?

Sally was worried. Wanda, her cat, was getting fat. She was behaving very strangely, too. She wouldn't go in her basket.

"She must be ill," Sally told her mummy. "Her tummy's all swollen, and she hasn't slept in her basket for days."

"Don't worry," said Mummy, giving Sally a hug. "If she's not better in the morning, we'll take her to the vet."

"Sssh!" whispered Sally. "You know how much Wanda hates the V-E-T." But it was too late, Wanda had already gone.

Sally and her mummy searched high and low but they couldn't find Wanda anywhere. She didn't even come running when they left out a saucer of milk.

Wanda was still missing the following morning.

"She must have heard us talking about the vet," said Sally, as they searched around the house.

They found all sorts of things they thought they had lost in the house, including Teddy, who was hiding under the sofa. But Wanda was nowhere to be seen.

"Perhaps she's hiding in the garden," said Sally.

They looked in the flowerbed, under the hedge, and up the tree. But all they found there were the birds.

"Sometimes she sunbathes in the vegetable patch," said Sally. But the only animal there was a fluffy rabbit.

"Wanda!" called Mummy, looking in the shed. Wanda often liked sleeping in there. But today all they found there were the mice.

"Maybe she's been locked in the garage," said Sally. So they found the keys and searched inside. They looked around the car. They looked in the car.

They even looked under the car. But all they found there were the spiders.

Wanda was nowhere around the house or garden, so Mummy took Sally to look in the park.

"Here, Wanda!" called Sally. But all they found there were dogs. Wanda hated dogs, so she wouldn't be there.

On the way home, they peeped over hedges and peered behind dustbins. Sally even sat on Mummy's shoulders so that she could look on top of people's garages and sheds. But Wanda was nowhere to be seen. She had disappeared.

"She must have run away," cried Sally. "We're never going to find her."

But Mummy had an idea. She helped Sally to draw some pictures of Wanda. Then they wrote MISSING and their telephone number on the pictures. They posted the leaflets through all the letterboxes in the street.

Later that afternoon, Sally and her mummy were sitting in the garden when Mrs Jones from next door popped her head over the hedge.

"Come and see what I've found in my laundry basket," smiled Mrs Jones.

Sally and her mummy rushed next door at once. When Sally saw what Mrs Jones had in her laundry basket she couldn't believe her eyes.

There, sitting amongst the washing, was Wanda. She looked very slim and very proud. And beside her lay five tiny kittens. They were so young that their eyes were still closed. Wanda hadn't been ill after all. She'd been expecting kittens!

Mrs Jones said that they could keep the basket until Wanda had finished with it. So Mummy carried the new family home as Sally skipped beside her.

Sally was so excited. She just couldn't wait to tell people how they'd gone searching for one cat and found six!

— Fierce — TIGER

Tiger wasn't really a tiger. He was a fierce stray kitten. People called him Tiger because he hissed and arched his back whenever they came near.

"You really should be nicer to people," said his friend Tibbles. "They're not so bad once you train them."

But Tiger didn't trust people. If they came too near, he would show his claws and even give them a scratch. That soon taught them not to mess with Tiger.

Tiger looked after himself. He didn't need anyone. At night he wandered the streets, searching dustbins for scraps and stealing food put out for pets. And during the day, he slept wherever he could – sometimes under a bush, sometimes on top of a garage, and sometimes under the cars in an old scrap yard.

One cold winter's night, Tiger was wandering the streets when it began to snow. He spotted an open window.

"Aha," thought Tiger. "I bet it's warm and dry in there." He jumped through the window and found himself in a dark porch.

"This will do," thought Tiger. So he curled into a ball

and was soon fast asleep. He was so comfortable that he slept all through the night.

When he finally woke up, there was no one around. But beside him was a bowl of food and a dish of water.

“Don’t mind if I do,” purred Tiger. He gobbled down the whole lot, then drank some water before leaving through the window again.

That day was colder than any Tiger had ever known, so when night fell and he saw the window open once more, he didn’t hesitate to sneak in. This time, Tiger could see that the door from the porch was slightly ajar. He pushed it open and found himself in a warm kitchen. So he settled down and had a wonderful night's sleep.

When he awoke in the morning, he found a bowl of delicious fish and a dish of water beside him.

"Don't mind if I do," purred Tiger. And he wolfed down the fish and lapped up the water before leaving.

That night it was still snowing. Tiger returned once more. This time, when he went to settle himself beside the fire, he found a cosy basket there.

"Don't mind if I do," purred Tiger. And he crawled in and went to sleep. Tiger had never slept so well.

In the morning, Tiger was woken by a rattling sound. Someone was in the kitchen.

Tiger opened his left eye just a crack. A little boy was placing a bowl beside the basket.

Tiger opened his eyes and stared at the little boy. The little boy stared at Tiger. Tiger leapt to his feet and got ready to hiss and scratch.

"Good boy," whispered the little boy, gently.

Tiger looked at the bowl. It was full of milk. "Don't mind if I do," he purred, and he drank the lot.

After that, Tiger returned to the house every night. Before long, he never slept anywhere else. The little boy always gave him plenty to eat and drink. And in return, Tiger let the little boy stroke him and hold him on his lap.

One morning, Tiger was playing with the little boy in the garden, when his old friend Tibbles strolled past.

"Hello Tiger," meowed Tibbles. "I thought you didn't like people!"

"Oh," smiled Tiger, "they're okay once you've trained them."

Tiger was no longer a fierce stray kitten!

— A Home — FOR ARCHIE

Archie, the black and white kitten, wasn't pleased. His owner, Tessa, hadn't given him his favourite fish for breakfast. All he had in his dish when he looked was some biscuits left over from the day before.

"Out you go," said Tessa, who was busy mopping the kitchen floor. And she pushed Archie out the door.

Now Archie was quite cross. He flicked his tail and swished his head. "I know when I'm not wanted," he thought. "I'll find someone who knows how to look after me!"

He jumped onto the garden fence and dropped into the neighbour's garden. Mrs Green always gave him a treat.

But as soon as his paws touched the ground, he heard a loud bark. Archie had forgotten about Bouncer, Mrs Green's playful new puppy.

Bouncer raced across the lawn and started to bounce around Archie.

"It's far too rough here," thought Archie, scrambling up a handy tree.

He jumped into the next garden. It belonged to Mr Reed. He didn't have a playful dog.

Archie strolled across the lawn and jumped up onto a window ledge. He was just about to squeeze through the open window, when he heard a squawk, followed by, "Who's a pretty boy?" Archie had forgotten about Mr Reed's parrot.

"It's far too noisy here," thought Archie. He made a quick escape through the hedge.

The next garden belonged to Granny Smith. She lived on her own and didn't have any pets.

"Meow!" called Archie. Granny Smith always had something nice to eat.

"Pussy!" cried a little voice from inside. Archie stopped in his tracks as he heard the patter of little feet running along the hall carpet. Oh, dear! Granny Smith's grandson was visiting. He always pulled Archie's tail. Archie decided to disappear before he got outside.

Archie squeezed through a broken panel in the fence. The next garden was rather overgrown. Some new people had just moved in and Archie hadn't met them yet. He hoped they liked kittens.

Archie strolled towards the house. He hadn't got far before he heard a hiss behind him. He turned around just in time to see a Siamese cat preparing to pounce. Archie, who knew better than to get in a fight with a Siamese, didn't stop to say hello. He flew through the grass, leapt onto the fence and ran as fast as his paws would carry him.

"I don't think I'll bother going there again," thought Archie, when he stopped for breath. He sat on the fence and thought what to do next. As he sat there, a wonderful fish smell drifted past. Archie sniffed and followed his nose, his tail twitching at the thought of a wonderful fish breakfast.

Archie wandered past garden after garden where children screamed, birds squawked, dogs barked and cats wailed. At last his nose gave an extra big twitch. He stopped by a garden that was wonderfully quiet.

"Archie, there you are!" a voice called. It was Tessa. "I've finished cleaning, and I've got a lovely piece of fish for you!"

Archie purred. "Good old Tessa!" he thought. "She does know how to look after me, after all!"

— Shanty — GOES TO SEA

Shanty, the harbour kitten, just loved fish. He ate every scrap that the fishermen threw away. And sometimes, when nobody was looking, he even helped himself to a few whole fish that should have gone to market.

"Don't you ever get tired of fish?" asked his friend Gull. But Shanty just shook his head and continued nibbling on a tasty sardine. He just couldn't get enough fish!

One day, Shanty had a brilliant idea. "There's only one thing that would be better than being a harbour kitten," he told Gull. "And that would be being a boat kitten. Then I could eat all the fish I wanted."

So the next morning, when none of the fishermen were looking, Shanty crept aboard the *Salty Sardine*, the biggest of all the fishing boats in the harbour. The sailors were so busy that they didn't notice the stowaway hidden beneath an old raincoat.

The sea was calm as the boat chugged out to sea, and Shanty had a great time dreaming about all the fish he was going to eat.

When the fishermen started pulling in the nets, Shanty couldn't believe his eyes. He was in kitten heaven. He'd never seen so many fish. There were mackerel. There were cod. There were haddock. And there were Shanty's favourite, sardines.

There were so many that nobody noticed when a few began to disappear under the old raincoat. And they didn't notice when the bones were thrown out the other side.

Shanty ate and ate, until he could eat no more. Then he curled up and settled down to sleep. But just as he was dozing off, something strange began to happen.

The *Salty Sardine* began to creak and moan. Then it began to sway and rock. Water sprayed over the sides as it bounced over the waves then crashed back down again. The *Salty Sardine* rode up and down the rough sea.

Shanty's head began to reel and his stomach began to roll. Oh, how he wished he hadn't eaten so many fish! Oh, how he wished he had stayed on dry land!

"We're going to drown," wailed Shanty, as a big wave crashed over him and the raincoat.

Soaked right through, Shanty peered out to see what the fishermen were doing. He couldn't believe his eyes. Instead of running about and screaming, they were carrying on with their work. One of them, who Shanty thought must be the captain, was even whistling. And another was eating a sausage roll. It seemed that for them, this was a normal day's work.

When the *Salty Sardine* finally got back to the harbour, Shanty couldn't get off fast enough.

"How is life as a boat kitten?" asked Gull, when he came visiting later that evening.

"Ah!" said Shanty, after he'd finished nibbling on a scrap of sardine. "Boats are all very well but give me the harbour any day. After all, how many fish can one kitten eat!"

Sparky and the BABY DRAGON

Sparky was a young dragon who lived in a cave far, far away. Now, as you know, dragons can breathe flames out of their noses! But you may not know that baby dragons have to *learn* how to do it.

"Watch me," said Mum to Sparky, and she puffed out a long flame and lit a candle.

"Now watch me," said Dad, and he breathed over some logs in the fireplace and made a fire. Sparky watched very carefully.

"Now watch *me*," he said, and he puffed until he was purple in the face. Two or three little sparks came out of his nose and ears!

"Bravo!" said Dad.

"It's coming on!" said Mum.

Sparky felt very proud.

One day Mum and Dad had to go out.

"Stay indoors," they told Sparky. "*Don't* go out, and *don't* let anybody in!"

"Why?" asked Sparky.

"Because of the wicked witch," said Mum. "She hates little dragons and turns them into teapots, just for fun!"

"Oh!" said Sparky. But he didn't mind staying in. He had some new toy knight figures to play with.

He had just started when he heard a bell outside.

"Ting-a-ling," it went, "ting-a-ling." And then a voice said, "Ice cream! Ice cream! Come and get your ice cream!"

Sparky peeped out. Outside was a brightly painted ice-cream cart. Sitting behind the wheel was an old woman with a big grin.

"Come and get your ice cream, Sparky," said the woman, and she laughed!

It was a loud, cackling laugh. When Sparky heard it, he knew it was the witch. He slammed the door and locked it.

The witch pedalled off in a rage.

"Phew!" thought Sparky, as he settled down to his knights and dragons game. "That was close."

The afternoon passed peacefully.

Then, the doorbell rang. "Who is it?" Sparky called out.

"It's Uncle Jack," said a voice, "I've come to take you fishing."

Sparky liked Uncle Jack, and he liked fishing! He went to open the door. Then he stopped.

"Is it really you?" he asked.

"Of course it is," laughed Uncle Jack.

But, as soon as Sparky heard the loud, cackling

laugh, he knew it was the witch.

"Go away!" he shouted. "Go away!"

Then he heard someone crying. He peered through the door and saw a baby dragon on the doorstep!

"I've lost my mummy!" sobbed the dragon.

"You'd better come in," said Sparky. He opened the door! The baby dragon rushed in! Then …

"Got you!" snapped the baby dragon. And turned into the witch!

Sparky gasped.

The witch raised her wand and shouted the magic word 'Ta-ra-ra-boom-de-ay!' and started to spin very fast.

Sparky closed his eyes and puffed as hard as he could. When he opened them he had a big surprise! The witch was surrounded by a puff of smoke.

Sparky watched in amazement as smoke cleared. Then, would you believe it, *she had turned herself into a teapot!*

Just then Mum and Dad came back.

"Have you had any trouble while we've been away?" asked Mum, kissing him.

"Not much!" said Sparky. "But, next time you go out, can I come with you?"

"Of course you can!" said Mum. "Now why don't I make some tea in this nice new teapot!"

BOINK

Boink was a small round monster. His name was Boink, but it was also the sound he made when he moved around. You and I can walk and run, but Boink the monster bounced like a ball – BOINK! BOINK! BOINK! – until he got where he was going. He looked like a space-hopper toy and he was rubbery too, to help him bounce.

Boink lived happily in an empty dog kennel at the bottom of Joe's garden. No one knew he was there. He couldn't even remember how he had got there, but that didn't worry him. Boink didn't worry about anything. He was a happy little monster and he enjoyed life. There was just one problem – he didn't have anything to play with.

Boink often watched Joe playing. Joe didn't have anyone to play with but he had lots of toys. Boink watched him as he took all his cars out of a big green box. He watched as he lined up all the red cars together, then all the blue cars, and then all the yellow cars. He watched as he moved the cars around. When Joe did this he made a strange sound.

"Brmmm! Brmmm!" he went, "Brmmm! Brmmm! Brmmm!"

Boink practised making the noise at night when no one was listening.

"Brmmm!" he said softly, and then louder, "Brmmm! Brmmm!" But it wasn't any fun without the cars. Boink wanted some toys of his own. So he decided to borrow some!

One night, when Joe was asleep, Boink bounced in through an open window. In Joe's bedroom there were toys everywhere. There were aeroplanes on a shelf and a train set on the floor. Boink took two cars out of the green box. Then he bounced out of the window and back to the dog kennel.

The first thing Joe noticed the next morning was that some of his cars were missing.

"Mum," he called, "have you seen my cars?"

But Joe's mum hadn't seen them. The next day Joe whizzed around the garden with his aeroplanes going, "Neeaw! Neeaw!"

Boink watched Joe playing, and that night he took two aeroplanes from Joe's bedroom!

"Mum," said Joe, going into the kitchen, "my aeroplanes are missing!"

"Did you leave them in the garden?" asked Mum. But Joe knew he hadn't. Joe had to play with his train set instead.

That night Joe only pretended to go to sleep. He couldn't believe his eyes! He saw a roly-poly monster

bounce in through the window and take his train set! As Boink bounced back out of the window Joe leapt out of bed and watched him disappear with the train set into the old kennel.

The next day, after breakfast, Joe went straight to the dog kennel and peeped inside. There, fast asleep, was a roly-poly monster. And all around him were Joe's missing toys! Joe was so surprised, he gave a startled yelp. Boink woke up.

"Brmmm! Brmmm!" said Boink grinning.

"What do you mean, Brmmm! Brmmm!?" said Joe.

"Neeaw! Neeaw!" said Boink.

"You only say Brmmm! Brmmm! when you're playing with cars," said Joe. "And you only say Neeaw! Neeaw! when you're playing aeroplanes."

"Neeaw! Neeaw!" said Boink.

"You can play with me if you like," said Joe, "but you must promise never to take my toys without asking."

"Chuff! Chuff!" said Boink.

"Right then, let's join up all the railway lines so that we can play with the train set," said Joe.

"Toot! Toot!" said Boink.

And that's what they did. When they had finished, the train set went in and out of the kennel and the engine went round and round.

When Joe's mum looked out of the window, she was pleased to see that Joe had found his missing toys. And she was surprised to see a space-hopper in the garden!

NESSY of the Lake

Nessy was a very shy monster. She was also very big. She was so big she could fill a swimming pool! Luckily, she lived in a large, deep lake, so no one ever saw her.

Nessy was too shy to go out and make friends. She once tried making friends with a small fish, but the fish bit her nose and swam away! Nessy shrugged. She was fed up. She hoped she'd find a friend soon.

One lovely sunny day Nessy peeped above the surface and saw a small boy fishing with his grandpa on the bank. The boy had a rod and a net and a shiny, red bucket.

He fished all day but didn't catch anything.

The next day Nessy watched again.

The little boy still didn't catch any fish.

"Watch out for ripples on the surface of the lake, Billy," said his grandpa. "Ripples mean fish!" Then Billy's grandpa nodded off to sleep.

Billy watched the surface of the lake for signs of ripples. Nessy watched Billy. All was quiet and still.

Then Nessy decided to go a bit closer … and closer … and closer still.

Billy stared at the ripples on the lake. He watched them coming closer … and closer … and closer still.

"Boo!" said Nessy suddenly splashing her head out of the water.

"Wow!" said Billy, staring. "You're not a fish – you're a monster!"

Nessy tried a friendly smile, showing all her teeth.

"Are you going to eat me?" asked Billy, alarmed.

"Of course not," said Nessy. "I want to be friends."

"You've got lots of big teeth," said Billy.

"Have I?" said Nessy. "Do they frighten you?"

"Not when you smile," said Billy.

Nessy smiled even wider.

"My name's Billy," said Billy. "What's yours?"

"Nessy," said Nessy. "What are you doing?" she asked Billy.

"I'm trying to catch a fish, but I'm not having much luck."

"I'll help," said Nessy. "Leave it to me!" and she started swimming very fast into the middle of the lake.

Then she disappeared! Billy stared at the middle of the lake. He stared for ages. Then the next thing he heard was Grandpa's voice saying, "Wake up, Billy!"

"I am awake," said Billy. "You'll never guess who I've been talking to, Grandpa!"

"Let me see," said Grandpa, "Old Mother Hubbard?"

"No," said Billy, "of course not."

"The Three Bears?"

"Grandpa!"

"Who then?"

"Nessy, of course, the monster who lives in the lake!"

"You've been dreaming, Billy!" smiled Grandpa.

"No I haven't," said Billy. "She came really close. And she splashed me, although she didn't mean to. Look ... my shoes are all wet!"

Grandpa looked.

"And she said she'd help me catch a fish," Billy went on.

"Well, it's time to go now,

Billy!" said Grandpa. "Don't forget your bucket!"

Billy picked up his bucket.

"Grandpa!" he said. "Look!"

Grandpa looked. There in Billy's bucket was the prettiest blue and gold fish he had ever seen.

"Well, I'll be blowed," said Grandpa.

Billy just grinned. Gently, he tipped the fish back into the water. Then he called out loudly, "See you, Nessy! See you tomorrow!"

And from the middle of the lake a big, shy monster waved back.

SNIFFLE

A long way away, in a jungle no one had ever been to before, lived the Sniffle monster.

The famous explorer, Major Jolly, went into the jungle looking for new animals. First, he found a big, bright bird that strutted about showing everyone what a great tail it had. Then he found a new type of monkey that could knit socks! His greatest discovery, though, was when he came upon the MONSTER, in a tree, eating a banana.

Major Jolly got very excited! The monster was intelligent! That means it could think like you and me. Major Jolly knew it was intelligent because only intelligent people eat bananas. Don't you think so? Well Major Jolly did, because he liked bananas too.

The monster was quite ugly, but then he would be, wouldn't he. He was big, ugly and covered in red fur. His fingertips could touch the floor when he was standing on the table!

Major Jolly decided to take him home to show his wife. They flew back in a big plane and the monster sat on three seats as well as a passenger. The famous explorer's wife met them at the airport.

"This is the monster I discovered, Maud," said Major Jolly. "He doesn't speak English."

"How do you do?" Maud held out her hand.

"Howdeedoodee," repeated the monster. He took the lady's hand and sniffed it, and then danced her round the room in circles.

"I'll soon have him speaking English," said Maud, as they danced past for the third time.

Back home the monster wanted to dance with everyone at first! But just a few weeks later he began to look ill and sad. He coughed and sniffed and spluttered. His coat turned dull, and patches of fur fell out. And he had something really nasty running out of his nose. He spent all day trying to lie on the sofa without falling off.

When Maud visited, he wouldn't dance round the room with her. "My dear Monster," she said, "what's wrong with you?"

The monster had learned to speak by now.

"I am Sniffle monster!" he said. "I was taken away from jungle without friend. I must have this friend with me always, or I get ill! Stuff comes out of my nose! My friend is Hanky monster."

Maud thought she understood.

"And you need this Hanky monster ... umm... to wipe your nose for you?"

"No, no, no!" said Sniffle. "Hanky is a magician. He will make Sniffle dance again! Only Hanky monster knows secret magic potion."

Major Jolly was really sorry that he had taken the Sniffle monster away from his Hanky monster. They must go back to the jungle straight away, find the Hanky monster, and Sniffle would be well again. Just a few days later, they found the place in the jungle where Major Jolly had camped before. Suddenly, something that looked like a giant cabbage hurtled through the bushes and threw itself at Sniffle. Sniffle gave a whoop of joy! The cabbage and Sniffle danced round the clearing until Sniffle was too tired to move. The cabbage was the Hanky monster, of course! It rushed back into the jungle.

"Gone to get magic potion," whispered Sniffle weakly.

The Hanky monster came back with a drink in a coconut shell. Sniffle drank it and went straight to bed. Next morning his coat was shiny and his nose had stopped running. He danced with everyone.

The secret potion was amazing! Sniffle was well again. Major Jolly was desperate to know the secret of the magic drink.

"It's a secret!" was all the Hanky monster would say. But when Major Jolly got home there was a letter for him with SECRET MAGIC POTION – DON'T TELL ANY PEOPLE! written on the outside. He opened the letter eagerly. A photograph of Sniffle and Hanky fell out. The letter read ...

HOT LEMON AND HONEY!

– The Fluff – MONSTERS

This is the story of the Fluff monsters. Everyone has seen fluff under the bed. That's because the Fluff monsters live under beds. They need beds that are not too clean underneath.

The Fluff monsters only come out when it's dark. They don't know what the world outside beds is like in daylight. They think it's scary just being out during the day. Who knows what might be out in the daylight? Once, Fluff-boy was having a quiet

meal eating fluff and custard, when suddenly *the-magic-sucking-thing* appeared. It made a terrible noise as it came closer and closer. Then a tube with a brush on the end sucked up all the fluff under the bed after he'd spent ages collecting it!

But Fluff-boy had only ever lived under his bed. He wanted to know what it was like under other beds.

"Only naughty Fluff monsters go out in daylight," said Fluff-mummy, "and do you know what happens to naughty Fluff monsters?"

"No, I don't," said Fluff-boy, alarmed. "What?"

His mother put on a scary voice and said, *"The Little Girl will get you!"*

Fluff-boy's eyes opened wide.

"Who's the Little Girl?" he asked.

"The Little Girl is a monster who lives *in the bed!"* said Fluff-mummy. "She is really clean and pretty! She will take you away and wash you and put you in a room with sun shining through the windows! She will open the doors and fill the room with fresh air from *outside!*"

"That's horrible! I don't believe you," said Fluff-boy. "You're making it up!"

"Well, you'll just have to be good," said Fluff-mummy, "or you'll find out!"

"Well, I'm not scared of the Little Girl!" said Fluff-boy.

Fluff-boy wasn't going to be put off. He wanted

to know what it was like under other beds. One day, while everyone was asleep, Fluff-boy slipped away. Outside, bright sunlight filled the room.

"That must be the window Fluff-mummy told me about," thought Fluff-boy.

He wandered into the next room and found another bed to slide under. There were spiders and daddy-long-legs, cobwebs and lots and lots of fluff! It was perfect! So Fluff-boy ate some fluff (though he did miss his mum's home-made custard) and settled into his new home.

But Fluff-boy couldn't sleep, as he was thinking about the Little Girl. He had to see if she was real or not. Plucking up courage he poked his head out from under the bed. Carefully, he climbed up the bed covers until he could scramble over the top.

Suddenly, the Little Girl woke and sat up. Fluff-boy was so surprised he jumped with fright.

"Aaargh!" shrieked Fluff-boy.

"Aaargh!" screamed the Little Girl.

They scrambled to each end of the bed and stared at each other.

"You gave me a fright!" said Fluff-boy.

"*Me* frighten *you*?" said the Little Girl. "*You* frightened *me!*"

"Did I?" said Fluff-boy. "Why?"

"Well, you're the Bogeyman aren't you?" said the Little Girl.

"There's no such thing as the Bogeyman,"

laughed Fluff-boy. "I'm Fluff-boy. I've just moved in under this bed. Do you live in this bed too?"

"No, silly," said the Little Girl. "I just sleep here at night. I thought scary Bogeymen lived under the bed. But you're not scary at all!"

"How about this then?" asked Fluff-boy. He stuck his thumbs in his ears, wiggled his fingers and poked his tongue out. The Little Girl laughed.

"That's not at all scary!" she said. "*This* is scary," and she pulled the corners of her mouth out with her fingers and crossed her eyes.

And that was how Fluff-boy and the Little Girl discovered that there is nothing scary under the bed or in it!

Wibble and the EARTHLINGS

Wibble was from the planet Xog. He was on a mission. He'd been sent secretly to Earth to find out about Earthlings.

Wibble's spaceship wobbled on landing, but there wasn't too much damage. He radioed back to Xog to tell them his camera was broken.

"Just tell us what the Earthlings look like," said Captain Pimples, the leader of the Xogs, "and I'll draw them. Over!"

"I will," said Wibble. "Over and out!" He climbed down from the spaceship and looked around. There was a big sign saying ZOO.

"I wonder what that means," thought Wibble.

Wibble wobbled over to the nearest building and opened the door. He went up to a big wooden fence and saw his first Earthling. With its long neck, it leaned over the fence and gave Wibble a huge lick.

"Calling Captain Pimples! Calling Captain Pimples!" Wibble yelled excitedly into his radio. "This Earthling is friendly and as tall as a tree! It has a long neck and little horns on its head! Over!"

Wibble read the sign on the pen. GIRAFFE. Wibble was looking at a giraffe, of course, but because he didn't understand the signs, Wibble thought it must be an Earthling. Captain Pimples drew an Earthling with a long neck and two horns.

"Sounds okay so far!" said the captain. "Tell me more. Over!"

Wibble wandered to the next fence, marked ELEPHANT. He switched on the radio.

"It's an enormous Earthling! It has huge ears and a long spout on the front like a teapot! Over!"

Captain Pimples quickly added the big ears and the spout to his drawing.

Next, Wibble went into a building marked AQUARIUM. He gazed around at the water tanks.

One had a sign that said SQUID. “This Earthling has two huge eyes and is covered in orange spots! Over!” Wibble said into his radio. Captain Pimples added two huge eyes and orange spots to the drawing.

“Okay!” said Captain Pimples. “We’ve heard enough. Earthlings are big and hairy, have enormous

ears and a spout, two huge eyes, and orange spots. A bit like us, really! Over and out!"

So Captain Pimples led an expedition to Earth. That is when Mr Brown the zoo-keeper walked by. Mr Brown got quite a shock when he saw them, but not half as much as the Xogs did when they saw him.

"Aargh!" cried the Xogs, running back to their spaceship. They took off and didn't stop until they reached planet Xog. Captain Pimples found Earth on his map, crossed it off and wrote underneath, "BEWARE—MONSTERS!"

Susie and the MERMAID

Today was Susie's birthday. Mum and Dad had given her a pretty sea-blue dress and shoes to match.

"Can I try them on now?" she asked.

"Of course, but don't get them dirty," warned her mum. Susie tried on the dress and shoes. They shimmered just like a mermaid's tail.

Susie had always wanted to be a mermaid. She wandered down to Mermaid Rock and gazed out to sea, dreaming of what it would be like to be a mermaid.

"I'll make a birthday wish,"

thought Susie to herself. She closed her eyes. "I wish I could be a mermaid."

When she opened her eyes, she was no longer wearing her birthday dress – she had a mermaid's tail! Susie couldn't believe her luck! Her birthday wish had come true.

But then Susie heard someone crying. She looked around. There was someone sitting on the other side of Mermaid Rock wearing a blue dress just like Susie's new birthday dress!

"Why are you crying?" Susie asked the little girl.

"I'm crying because I've lost my tail," she replied. "You see, I'm a mermaid. But without my tail I can't go home!" As the mermaid cried, her tears splashed into the sea.

Susie suddenly realised what had happened. Her birthday wish must have made her swap places with the mermaid. Susie told the mermaid about her birthday wish.

"What can I do to change us back again?" asked Susie.

"If you can collect my tears from the sea, then you could wish again," said the mermaid.

Susie slipped into the sea. The water didn't feel a bit cold now that she was a mermaid. With her strong new tail she swam quickly to the bottom of the sea. But Susie didn't have any idea how to look for the mermaid's tears!

Susie asked the sea creatures to help her search for the tears. Crabs and fish, lobsters and winkles peered into holes and lifted up stones, but it was no use. They couldn't find a single tear. Susie didn't know what to do!

Then she heard, "One-two-three, one-two-three..." and from an underwater cave danced a large octopus wearing a long

string of pearls! Its eight long arms whirled around as the octopus danced and twirled.

"Hello, little mermaid!" said the octopus.

"Can you help me?" asked Susie. "I'm looking for mermaid tears. But I don't know where to start."

"Ah! Well these pearls are just what you are looking for!" said the octopus. "That's what happens to mermaid tears you know – they turn into pearls! You can have them if you help me take them off!" laughed the octopus.

"Oh, thank you so much!" cried Susie untangling the pearls.

"Farewell, little mermaid!" laughed the octopus as it danced away, singing, "One-two-three, one-two-three ..."

Susie swam back to Mermaid Rock as quickly as

she could with the pearls. The mermaid was overjoyed. Susie closed her eyes and wished again. Instantly, she was wearing her blue dress and the mermaid had her tail back.

"Thank you, Susie," said the mermaid. "I hope I'll see you again."

Susie waved goodbye as the mermaid slipped into the sea and swam away. Susie hurried home for her birthday tea. She glanced down at her new blue dress to make sure it was still clean. Around the dress were sewn lots of tiny tear-shaped pearls!

Jade and the JEWELS

Jade was the prettiest mermaid in the lagoon! Her hair was jet black and reached right down to the tip of her swishy, fishy tail. Her eyes were as green as emeralds, and her skin was as white as the whitest pearl. But Jade was so big-headed and vain that the other mermaids didn't like her!

"That Jade thinks too much of herself!" the other mermaids would say. "One of these days she'll come unstuck!"

There was one creature, though, who was fond of Jade, and that was Gentle, the giant turtle. He followed her wherever she went.

But Jade didn't even notice Gentle. She lived in a world of her own. She spent all her time combing her hair and admiring her reflection in the mirror.

One day Jade overheard the mermaids talking about a pirate ship that had sunk to the bottom of the ocean. On board was a treasure chest filled with precious jewels.

"But no one dares take the jewels," whispered the mermaids, "because the pirate ship is cursed!"

“I’m going to find that pirate ship,” Jade told Gentle, “and the treasure chest!”

“But what about the curse?” asked Gentle.

“Oh, never mind that. Just imagine how beautiful I will look wearing all those jewels!” said Jade, and right away she set off.

“Wait for me!” called Gentle, paddling after her. “It’s too dangerous to go alone!”

Jade swam to a deep part of the ocean she had never been to before. She dived through shoals of colourful fish, past the edge of the coral reef and deep, deep down to the very bottom of the ocean.

Finally, they found the shipwreck.

"Be careful, Jade," said Gentle. "Remember there is a curse on this pirate wreck."

"Nonsense," Jade told him. "I've come to get the jewels and I'm not going home without them!"

Jade searched the wreck until she saw the treasure chest through a porthole. Jade swam inside and reached out to touch the chest. The lid sprang open and brilliant jewels spilled over the sides. The colours were dazzling.

Jade lifted out a necklace and put it round her neck. There was a little gold and silver mirror in the chest. She held it up to admire her reflection. The necklace was beautiful! Jade looked lovelier than ever.

Suddenly, there was a loud crack, and the mirror shattered! Instantly the necklace turned to stone! It was the ship's curse!

Jade tried to take the necklace off, but she couldn't. She tried to swim, but the necklace was so heavy she couldn't move.

"Help!" Jade cried out. "Help! Help!" Gentle, the giant turtle, heard her and swam to the porthole.

"Help me, Gentle," she cried. "Please help me!"

"I warned you to be careful," said Gentle.

Jade began to cry. "I should have listened to you, Gentle," she sobbed.

Gentle's powerful flippers broke the necklace and freed Jade. As Jade and Gentle swam away from the wreck, Gentle said, "You don't need fancy jewels, Jade. You're pretty without them."

Once she was safely home, Jade told the other mermaids about the pirate ship curse.

"I've certainly learned my lesson," said Jade. "I'll never be vain again." And, from that day on, they were all friends. But Gentle was always her very best friend of all.

The Naughty MERMAIDS

Of all the mermaids that lived in the sea, Jazz and Cassandra were the naughtiest. They were not supposed to swim above sea when there were people about. But their latest prank was to swim to the lighthouse and call out to the little boy who lived there.

"Coo-ee!" they would call and, when the little boy looked towards them, they giggled and dived under the waves.

"Coo-ee!" they called again from the other side of the lighthouse. Just as he ran round to see them, they dived under the waves again!

When King Neptune heard about it, he was very cross indeed!

"I won't have this naughty behaviour," he boomed. "Mermaids should not mix with children!"

But Jack, that was the boy's name, was lonely at the lighthouse. There was no one to play with. One day, Jack's mum made him a picnic. Jack laid the food on a cloth on the rocks. He had pizza and crisps and fizzy drink and chocolate.

The two naughty mermaids popped up from the waves. They soon spotted all the food.

"Hello!" they called to Jack. "Are you going to eat all this food by yourself?"

Jack was so surprised that he couldn't speak. He'd never seen the mermaids before.

"Yes," said Jack, at last. "I mean, no! You can have some of my picnic, if you like."

The mermaids had never had pizza or crisps or fizzy drink or chocolate before. They ate so much they felt quite sick! They swam home slowly, hoping King Neptune wouldn't spot them. But he did! And he summoned them to come and see him.

"Be warned!" said King Neptune. "Mermaids are not like children. They cannot behave like children and they cannot eat the food that children eat!"

For a while Jazz and Cassandra played with the other ocean creatures and ate mermaid food, like shrimps and seaweed. But they soon became bored!

"I'm longing for some pizza," said Jazz to Cassandra one day.

"So am I," answered Cassandra, "and some of those crispy things."

"Mmmm, and fizzy stuff!"

"And chocolate!"

The naughty mermaids looked at each other! Then, holding hands they swam up to the surface.

Jack was waiting for them with a picnic all ready. They ate and ate and ate. It all tasted so good. Afterwards they played hide-and -seek in the waves while Jack ran round the lighthouse trying to spot them. The mermaids enjoyed themselves so much, they came back the next day and the next.

On the third day, the mermaids said goodbye and started to swim to the bottom of the sea. But, oh dear! Their tails had become stiff and heavy. They could not move! King Neptune was right! Mermaids can't behave like children. They clung onto the rocks around the lighthouse and began to cry.

"What's wrong?" shouted Jack, alarmed.

"We're not supposed to eat children's food," they told him.

Jack knew exactly what to do! He got his net and bucket and searched the island, collecting shrimps and seaweed from the rock pools.

For three days and three nights he fed the mermaids proper mermaid food. By the end of the third day they could move their tails again and swim.

When they arrived home King Neptune was waiting for them. This time, King Neptune wasn't angry – he was glad to see them back safely.

"I hope you have learned a lesson," he said, quite gently. "Jack has been a good friend so you can play with him again. As long as you don't eat his food!"

From then on they saw quite a lot of their friend Jack, often going up to talk and play with him. But they never again ate Jack's food, except sometimes they had a piece of chocolate!

The Mermaid IN THE POOL

John and Julia were on holiday at the seaside. Their mum and dad had found an amazing house with a big swimming pool. But, best of all, their bedroom overlooked the beach. It was perfect!

The first night there was a storm. The wind howled. The waves crashed over the beach and right up to the house. The children lay in bed listening to the storm outside.

By morning, the storm was over. The children woke early and looked out of their window. The garden furniture had blown over, there was seaweed all over the lawn and there was a mermaid in the swimming pool!

That's right! There was a mermaid in the swimming pool! The mermaid was swimming up and down the pool. John and Julia rushed outside but, when the mermaid saw them coming, she huddled in a corner of the pool. She was frightened.

"I'm sorry I swam into your blue pool," said the mermaid. "I didn't mean any harm!"

"It's okay!" said Julia gently. "We didn't mean to frighten you."

"That's right," said John. "We just wanted to meet you. We've never seen a mermaid before."

"My name is Marina," said the mermaid. "I was playing in the sea with my friend Blue, the dolphin, when the storm began. A huge wave washed me in, and now I'm stranded, and Blue is missing!"

"We'll help you look for Blue," said Julia at once. "We might be able to spot your friend from our bedroom window."

As soon as their mum and dad were safely out of the way, John and Julia found a wheelbarrow and wheeled Marina into the house.

"I've only had sky over my head before," said Marina. "The house won't fall on me will it?"

"Of course not," smiled John. They showed Marina all sorts of things she had never seen before. She thought the moving pictures on the television were weird. She thought Julia's teddy bear was wonderful, and that beds were the silliest things she had ever seen!

But, although they looked out of the window, there was no sign of Blue the dolphin in the sea.

"I have to go home soon!" Marina said sadly. "I can't stay out of the water for long, and I must find Blue. If only I hadn't lost my shell horn in the storm I could call him."

"We'll take you down to the sea," said John.

"And help you look for your shell," said Julia.

They lifted Marina back into the wheelbarrow and pushed her down to the beach. They spent the rest of the day searching for Marina's shell along the seashore. They had almost given up when, suddenly, Julia spotted a large shell half buried in the sand. John found a stick and dug it out. "It's my shell!"

cried Marina. They washed off the sand and Marina blew into it. The most beautiful sound drifted out across the waves. Straight away, there was an answering call! Far out to sea, they saw a streak of blue-grey. It was leaping high over the waves, swimming towards them. It was Blue, the dolphin!

Marina gave a cry of joy and swam to meet him. She flung her arms round his neck and hugged him. Then she turned to the watching children.

"Thank you for helping me," she called.

"See you next year!" called John and Julia. And they watched as Marina and Blue swam swiftly and smoothly together, back out to sea.

King Neptune's DAY OFF

Trini the little mermaid worked in King Neptune's palace. It was a beautiful palace, with fountains and a statue of King Neptune in the centre of the courtyard. Trini was happy working there. But some fierce sharks guarded the palace.

Today it was King Neptune's birthday. King

Neptune called Trini to see him.

"I'm taking the day off," he said. "I'd like you to organise a birthday banquet for me this evening when I come back. So, until then, you will be in charge." And off he went!

The sharks were delighted! They thought they would have some fun while King Neptune was away.

"I'm in charge, so you must do as I say," Trini told them sternly, after the king had left.

The sharks just sniggered at her and didn't answer.

Trini set to work. She asked a team of fish to collect shrimps and special juicy seaweed. She told the crabs to collect smooth, pearly shells to use as plates. Then she sent her mermaid friends to collect pieces of coral to decorate the tables.

But the sharks were determined to make mischief and spoil everything. Before long they saw the fish carrying a net full of delicious food. "Give us that," they snapped, and in a few gulps the food was gone.

As soon as the crabs came back with their shell plates, the sharks took the shells and began throwing them to each other.

"Stop it at once!" cried Trini. But the sharks ignored her.

Then the sharks spotted the mermaids watching close by. They started to chase them all around the courtyard. "Stop it!" cried Trini. But the sharks just laughed and carried on chasing the mermaids.

Then Trini had an idea. She would trick the sharks! While they were chasing the mermaids, Trini squeezed through a crack in the hollow statue of King Neptune. The sharks were having great fun. The mermaids dropped all their pretty coral and swam away. The sharks couldn't stop laughing.

They gathered around King Neptune's statue to plan some more mischief.

Suddenly, a voice like thunder boomed, "Behold, it is I, King Neptune, Emperor of all the Seas and Oceans." The sharks were very frightened. Then the voice bellowed, "Do as Trini commands or you will be banished from the kingdom!"

Then the voice from inside the statue told the sharks to pick up the plates and fetch more food and lay the tables for the banquet. And, while they were busy, Trini crept out from inside the hollow statue where she had been hiding!

So Trini's banquet was a great success. Everyone was there, even the sharks! But they had to stand guard outside the palace, while everyone inside enjoyed the food, music and dancing. King Neptune had a marvellous time and asked Trini if she would always be his special helper.

"I'd be delighted," she answered, blushing!

The Clumsy FAIRY

Did you know that all fairies have to go to school to learn *how* to be fairies? Well they do! They have to learn how to fly, how to be graceful and how to do magic. Some fairies find it difficult. Clementine did!

Poor Clementine. She was the worst in the class. She was clumsy and awkward. When they were dancing she was the only fairy who tripped over her own feet.

"Clementine! Think of feathers, not elephants,"

Madame Bouquet, the fairy dance teacher, was forever saying.

At the end of term all the fairies were given a special task for the holidays. Sweetpea and Beatrice had to make garlands of flowers for the May Ball. Jemima and Poppy had to collect honey from the bees. Breeze and Scarlet had to polish the leaves on the holly tree.

But there was one task that no one wanted. This was to help a little girl who had measles.

"Clementine," said Madame Bouquet, "I want you to take this rose petal lotion, and paint it on the little girl's spots when she is asleep," said Madame Bouquet. "If you do this every night, for one whole week, the spots will disappear."

Clementine couldn't wait to start. That night she flew to the little girl's house and in through the bedroom window. So far so good! The little girl's name was Alice, and Clementine could see her fast asleep in bed. She was holding a fat, round teddy in her arms.

Clementine crept towards the bed. Then she tripped over the rug and sat on a prickly hairbrush which was lying on the floor.

"Ouch!" she yelled.

Alice stirred, but didn't wake. Clementine got up quietly. She bent over to pick up the hairbrush, and a toy clown, with a silly face, pinched her bottom!

"Ouch!" she yelled again.

This time Alice did wake up. "Who's there?" she asked sleepily.

"It's Clementine," said the fairy, "and your clown just pinched my bottom!"

"Never did!" said the clown.

"Are you sure?" Alice asked Clementine, rubbing her eyes. "He's usually very well behaved."

Then Clementine overbalanced and sat down quickly on Alice's hot-water bottle which was lying on the floor. It was so bouncy that she shot straight up in the air and landed with a plop on Alice's bed.

"Are you alright?" asked Alice, rubbing her eyes again, to make sure she wasn't seeing things.

Clementine smoothed her crumpled dress and fluttered her wings. She explained to Alice why she had come.

"I'm sorry I woke you," she added. "You're not really supposed to see me."

Alice didn't mind. She thought it was lovely to be able to talk to a real fairy.

"Can you really do magic?" she asked Clementine.

"Yes," Clementine told her. "I'm quite good at magic. I just wish I wasn't so clumsy."

She told Alice about her dance classes and Alice told Clementine about her ballet lessons.

"If you are helping me get rid of my measles," she said to Clementine, "I'll help you with your ballet."

So each night Clementine went to see Alice. Alice taught Clementine how to point her toes, how to keep her balance on one foot and how to curtsy gracefully. Clementine worked hard to copy everything Alice showed her. But it was the pirouette that Clementine did best of all. Holding her arms high above her head she twirled and twirled round Alice's bedroom.

In return, Clementine painted Alice's spots. Each day they became fainter and fainter. By the end of the week they had gone.

After the holidays the fairies went back to school.

"Now fairies," said Madame Bouquet, "I want you to show me *The Dance of the Sugar Plum Fairy.*"

The music started and the fairies began to dance. And, do you know, Clementine was the best dancer in the class. Madame Bouquet couldn't believe her eyes.

"Why, Clementine," she gasped, "you're my prima ballerina!"

And 'prima', as I'm sure you know, means 'first and best'!

Clementine was the happiest fairy in the world!

Sugarplum - and the - BUTTERFLY

Sugarplum," said the Fairy Queen, "I've got a very important job for you to do."

Sugarplum was always given the most important work. The Fairy Queen said it was because she was the kindest and most helpful of all the fairies.

"I want you to make a rose-petal ball gown for my birthday ball next week."

"It will be my pleasure," said Sugarplum happily. She liked being busy.

She set to work straight away. Sugarplum began to gather cobwebs to make the thread, and rose petals to make the dress. While she was collecting the thread she found a butterfly caught in a cobweb.

"Oh, you poor thing," sighed Sugarplum. She stopped what she was doing to help him. Very carefully, Sugarplum untangled the butterfly. But his wing was broken. Sugarplum laid the butterfly on a bed of feathers.

He was very sick and weak with hunger. Sugarplum gathered some nectar from a special flower and fed him a drop at a time. Then she set about mending his wing with a magic spell. Every day Sugarplum fed the butterfly with nectar and cast her spell to mend his wing. After six days, the butterfly was better. He was very grateful. But by now Sugarplum was behind with her work!

"I shall never finish the Fairy Queen's ball gown by tomorrow," she cried. "Whatever shall I do?"

The butterfly comforted her.

"Don't worry, Sugarplum," he said. "We will help you." He gathered all his friends together. There were yellow butterflies, blue butterflies, red and brown butterflies. He told them how Sugarplum had rescued him from the cobweb and helped to mend his wing. The butterflies gladly gathered up lots of rose petals and dropped them next to Sugarplum. Then the butterflies flew away to gather more cobwebs, while Sugarplum arranged all the petals.

Back and forth went Sugarplum's hand with her needle and thread making the finest cobweb stitches. Sugarplum added satin ribbons and bows. When she had finished, Sugarplum was very pleased.

"Dear friend," she said to the butterfly, "I couldn't have finished the dress without your help."

"And I couldn't have flown again without your kindness," said the butterfly.

The Fairy Queen was delighted with her new ball gown. And, when she heard the butterfly's story, she wrote a special 'Thank You' poem for Sugarplum:

Sugarplum is helpful,
Sugarplum is kind.
Sugarplum works hard all day,
But she doesn't mind.
She always does her very best,
To make sick creatures well.
She brings such joy and pleasure
As she weaves her magic spell!

The FOOTBALL Fairy

Georgina loved to play football. But there was just one problem.

"I'm fed up with these silly wings," she said, wiggling her shoulders. "They just get in the way."

The other fairies didn't agree at all.

"Whoever heard of a fairy without wings?" laughed Twinkletoes, doing a little dance.

"You wouldn't be able to fly if you didn't have wings," said Petal, landing on a flower.

"Flying is brilliant," called Sparkle, sprinkling fairy dust.

"Keep that fairy dust away from me," sneezed Georgina crossly. "I'm going to play football."

"Football is a game for elves, not fairies!" said Sparkle.

"In that case, I don't want to be a fairy!" said Georgina, and stamped off.

"She'll change her mind," said the wise fairy, "just wait and see."

But Georgina wouldn't change her mind. She pulled on her football boots and went to play with the elves.

The football game was very rough. The ball bounced around the field and, quite often, off the field! Sometimes it went up into the trees. Two birds who were trying to build their nest got very fed up, especially when the football landed near them.

Georgina flew up to get it. "Perhaps my wings can be useful after all," she thought, landing on the ground. She looked round quickly, hoping no one had seen her.

But someone had! Barry, the elf, was a tell-tale! He couldn't wait to tell the fairies what he had seen.

"Ah," nodded the wise fairy. "I knew she would use her wings sooner or later." But Georgina still wouldn't join in with the other fairies.

The next time she played football, the game was

rougher than ever. One elf kicked the ball so hard it flew into the tree and hit the birds' nest. This time there was an egg in it! The egg began to topple. None of the elves noticed; they were far too busy arguing with the referee. So Georgina flew up and, just in time, caught the egg before it hit the ground. Then she flew up to the nest.

"Thank you," said the mummy bird, rather sternly, tucking the egg back under her. "But please, in future, be more careful when you play football!"

Georgina promised she would.

When she flew down from the tree, Barry the tell-tale elf saw her. Of course, he told the fairies. They looked knowingly towards Georgina. "What did I tell you?" said the wise fairy. "She'll soon come round to being one of us."

Next time she played football, Georgina checked the tree first. The mummy bird was away. "Good!" she thought. "She can't complain this time." But, thanks to a naughty elf, the football knocked into the birds' nest. A small bundle of feathers tumbled out. It was a baby bird!

Georgina spotted it and, quick as lightning, she flew up to catch him. Gently, she held him in her arms and flew back to the nest. When he was safely inside she sprinkled him with fairy dust to keep him from further harm. Just then mummy bird came back.

"I shall tell everyone about your kindness," she said, as her baby snuggled under her feathers. "And, as you're such a good fairy, will you be baby Beak's godmother?"

"I'd be delighted!" said Georgina.

When they heard the news, the other fairies were very proud of her.

"Perhaps it's not so bad being a fairy after all," grinned Georgina.

– The Tooth – FAIRY

Pansy was nearly five. She couldn't wait for her birthday because Mum had promised her a party in the garden. There would be birthday cake and balloons and a funny clown. All her friends were coming to her party.

There was only one problem! Pansy's two front teeth were loose. They wobbled whenever she bit into anything. How was she going to enjoy her party food?

"Mum," she asked, for the

hundredth time, "will my wobbly teeth come out before my birthday party?"

"They'll come out when they're ready," said Mum, smiling.

That night Pansy woke suddenly. The curtains were open and her bed was covered in silvery moonlight. But that wasn't all! Sitting on Pansy's pillow was ... can you guess? A fairy! It's true! She was tiny, with pale yellow wings, a wand and a sparkly dress.

Pansy could hardly believe it. She stared at the fairy, and the fairy stared back at her. The fairy spoke first.

"Can you see me?" she asked.

"Yes," said Pansy.

"That's funny," said the little fairy. "Usually I'm invisible!"

"Are you the tooth fairy?" asked Pansy.

"Yes, I'm Bobo," said the fairy. "I need two tiny front teeth to replace the keys on my piano."

Pansy showed Bobo her two front teeth. They were *very* wobbly.

"I hope they come out before my birthday party," said Pansy.

"They'll come out when they are ready," said Bobo. "If they come out before your birthday, I'll play my piano at your party!"

The next day, Bobo peeped into the playroom and found Pansy standing on her head!

"What are you doing, Pansy?" she asked.

"If I stay like this all day," said Pansy, "my teeth might fall out."

At teatime Bobo watched from behind a bowl of fruit, as Pansy ate all her cheese on toast, including the crusts. But still her teeth didn't come out!

"Try brushing your teeth," Bobo whispered to her, before Pansy went to bed.

"Oh yes! That will do it!" said Pansy. And she brushed and brushed and brushed, but the wobbly teeth just stayed stubbornly in her mouth.

The day before Pansy's birthday her two front teeth came out! It didn't hurt one little bit.

"Look!" she said to Mum, pulling a face, and showing a big gap where her teeth should be.

"Scary! Scary!" laughed Mum, pretending to be frightened.

"These are for Bobo," said Pansy, showing Mum the teeth.

"Who's Bobo?" asked Mum.

"The tooth fairy, of course," said Pansy.

That night Pansy went to bed early. She put her teeth under the pillow.

"I'll just close my eyes for a minute," she said to herself, "but I won't go to sleep."

Later Bobo came in, but Pansy had already dozed off. Bobo even whispered Pansy's name, but Pansy was fast asleep.

Pansy didn't wake until the sun shone through her curtains the next morning. The first thing she did was look under the pillow. The two tiny teeth had gone! In their place were two coins.

Pansy's fifth birthday party was the best she'd *ever* had. All her friends came. There was jelly and ice cream, balloons and the funniest clown she'd ever seen.

Her friends sang 'Happy Birthday' so loudly that Mum had to put her fingers in her ears. But only Pansy could see the tiny fairy playing a piano and singing 'Happy Birthday' in a silvery voice.

The Yellow BLUEBELLS

The fairies at Corner Cottage were always busy. The garden was full of flowers and it was the fairies' job to look after them. You never saw them because they worked at night and hid during the day.

Blossom, the youngest fairy, was also one of

the busiest. It was her job to paint all the bluebells.

Corner Cottage had a lot of bluebells. They spread out under the apple tree like a deep blue carpet.

One evening, Blossom was sick.

"I've got a terrible cold," she told her friend Petal, sniffing loudly. "I don't think I can work tonight."

"I wish I could help," said Petal, "but I've got to spray the flowers with perfume or they won't smell right. You'll have to ask the gnomes."

Oh dear! Nobody liked asking Chip and Chuck, the garden gnomes. All they liked doing was fishing and windsurfing on the pond and playing tricks. Blossom was very worried about asking them.

"No problem!" said Chip and Chuck when she asked them. "Just leave it to us."

But Blossom was right to worry! When she got up the next morning the gnomes had painted some of the bluebells ... YELLOW! She couldn't believe it.

"Have you seen what they've done?" she said to Petal. "What will Jamie think?"

Jamie lived in Corner Cottage with his mum and dad, and he played in the garden every day. That morning he came out as usual and made for the apple tree. It was a great tree for climbing. As he sat on his favourite branch, he looked down. Something looked different.

"I'm sure those flowers were blue yesterday," he thought.

"Mum," he said, going into the kitchen, "I've picked you some flowers."

"Yellowbells?" said Mum, putting them into a jam jar. "Where did you get these?"

"Under the apple tree," said Jamie.

"How odd," said Mum. "I don't remember planting those."

That night, Blossom was still feeling ill.

"You'll have to paint the yellowbells again," she told the gnomes. But Chip and Chuck just chuckled.

In the morning, Jamie ran out to the garden and climbed the apple tree. This time the flowers were pink! He picked a bunch for his mum and she put them in the jam jar with the yellowbells.

When Petal told Blossom what had

happened, Blossom groaned.

"I just knew something like this would happen." But she was still feeling too sick to work.

"Don't worry," said Petal. "Leave it to me." Petal made the naughty gnomes paint all the pinkbells again.

And this time she watched them carefully. The naughty gnomes grumbled loudly.

"Do it," said Petal, "or you'll never fish or windsurf on the pond again!"

The next morning, all the bluebells were blue again. Blossom was feeling much better.

"I'll be glad to get back to work!" she told Petal.

When Jamie and his mum went into the garden,

everything was as it should be. The bluebells were the right colour. And there was no sign of the yellowbells or pinkbells.

"It must have been the fairies!" joked Mum.

That night, as Jamie lay in bed he heard laughing and splashing from the fishpond. But, when Jamie peered through window, he couldn't see anything.

"Maybe it really was the fairies," he thought as he drifted off to sleep.

— Princess — ROSEBUD

In a beautiful palace in a land far away, lived a little princess. The king and queen called her Princess Rosebud, because on her left ankle was a small pink mark in the shape of a rose.

On her third birthday, Princess Rosebud was given a pretty white pony. The princess rode her pony with her nanny and her groom at her side. They went to the edge of the forest then stopped for a rest. The pretty white pony was tied to a tree branch. The nanny and the groom talked

together, while the little princess wandered along a forest path collecting flowers and leaves. They didn't notice how far the little princess had wandered. Soon Princess Rosebud couldn't see her nanny or her groom or her beautiful white pony. She called and called for her nanny. But no one came. It began to get dark. The little princess was scared and began to cry.

Princess Rosebud walked on until she saw a light through the trees. There was a little house with a straw roof and tiny little windows and a small wooden door. Suddenly, the door opened. There stood a little old woman!

Now, the old woman was blind and couldn't see the little princess, but she could hear a small child crying.

The old woman was kind. She took the little princess inside and sat her by a warm fire. Then she gave her thin slices of bread and honey, and a glass of milk.

"What is your name, child?" she asked.

"Rosebud," answered the princess.

"Where do you live, child?" she asked.

"I don't know," answered the princess. "I got lost in the forest."

"Well, you can stay with me until someone comes to find you, my dear," said the kind old woman.

Back at the palace, the king and queen were very upset that their only daughter was lost. They offered a reward of a hundred gold coins to anyone who

could find her. But many years went by and no one found the little princess. The king and queen thought they would never see the princess again.

Meanwhile Rosebud was very happy living in the forest. She forgot that she had ever been a princess! She forgot she had lived in a palace! She forgot her fine clothes and jewels. She even forgot her white pony!

One day, when she was walking in the garden, a pony galloped into view. He was as white as milk, and had a jewelled saddle and bridle!

Rosebud loved him immediately! She climbed into the saddle, and the pony turned swiftly, and galloped off! He took her to the palace gate. Rosebud felt she had seen the palace before, but could not remember when. Before dark, the pony returned her to the cottage in the forest.

The next day he came again, and again they visited the palace before returning to the cottage.

Then the next day, the palace gate was open. The pony trotted through the gate just as the king and queen were walking in the gardens. They saw the little girl and the pony and thought she was the prettiest girl they had ever seen.

"What is your name, child?" the queen asked her.

"Rosebud, your majesty," Rosebud replied.

"Ah," sighed the queen sadly, "that is the name of my long-lost daughter."

Then, just as Rosebud was mounting the pony to ride home, the queen noticed the pink rose on her left ankle!

She stared at it in disbelief!

"Sire!" she cried to the king. "It is our daughter, Princess Rosebud."

The whole kingdom rejoiced to hear that the princess had returned. The king offered the old woman a reward for caring for the princess, but she shook her head.

"I only want to be near Rosebud for the rest of my days," she said. And so the old woman came to live in the palace with Princess Rosebud.

The Pig and THE JEWELS

Daisy was as pretty as a picture. She was very kind too. Daisy looked after all the animals on the farm where she lived. She loved them all dearly, and the animals all loved her too.

But Daisy dreamt of being more than a farmer's daughter. As she fed the hens and the ducks or counted the sheep, Daisy day-dreamed about being a princess. At night when she lay in bed she would say to herself, "Oh, how I wish I could be a princess!"

One day she found a sick pig

at the edge of the forest. She carried him to the farm and nursed him until he was better. The pig became her favourite animal, and he followed her wherever she went.

She told him all her secrets, and he listened carefully, his little eyes fixed on hers. It was almost as if he understood everything she said. She even told him the most important secret of all.

"Dear little pig," she whispered in his ear, " I wish, I wish I could be a princess!"

That night the pig went away. When he returned the next morning, he had a tiara made of precious jewels on his head. The pig stood in front of Daisy, the jewels glinting in the sunshine.

"Darling pig," cried Daisy, "is that for me?"

The pig grunted. Daisy took the tiara and put it on her head. It fitted her perfectly.

The next night the pig went away again. In the morning he returned as before, this time with a beautiful necklace. Daisy put it on.

"How do I look?" she asked him. But of course the pig just grunted.

After that the pig went away every night for six nights. And every morning for six mornings he returned with something different.

First he brought a dress of white silk, followed by

a crimson cloak and soft leather shoes. Then bracelets set with jewels, and long lengths of satin ribbon for her hair. And, finally, a ring made of gold and rubies.

Daisy put on all the gifts the pig had brought her and stood in front of a long mirror.

"At last," she whispered to her reflection, "I look just like a real princess."

The next day the pig disappeared again. Daisy didn't worry because she knew he always returned. But days went by and then weeks, and the pig did not return. Daisy missed him more than she could say.

Summer turned to autumn, and autumn to winter. The days grew short and snow lay in deep drifts on the ground. Daisy spent the evenings sitting by the fire in her white silk dress and crimson cloak. Her heart was sad and heavy when she thought about her dear, lost pig.

"I would be happy just to remain a farmer's daughter if only he would return to me," she cried, watching the logs burn in the hearth.

Suddenly there was a noise at the door – it was the pig! With a cry of joy she bent to kiss him and, as she did, he turned into a handsome prince!

Daisy gasped with amazement.

"Sweet Daisy," said the prince taking her hand. "If it wasn't for you I would still be alone and friendless, wandering in the forest."

He explained how a wicked witch had cast a spell on him to turn him into a pig. "Your kiss broke the spell," said the prince. "Daisy, will you marry me?"

It was a dream come true. At long last, Daisy really was going to become Princess Daisy!

The PRINCESS Who Never Smiled

A long time ago, in a far-off land, a princess was born. The king and queen called her Princess Columbine. They thought she was the most precious child ever to be born. And, to make sure that she was watched over every minute of every day, they hired a nurse to look after her.

One day, the queen came to the nursery and found the nurse asleep and the little princess crying. The queen was very cross and called for the king. He told off the nurse for not watching the baby.

But what the king and queen didn't know was that the nurse was really a wicked enchantress. The angry enchantress cast a spell over the little baby princess:

"Princess Columbine will never smile again until she learns my real name!"

The king and queen were devastated. From that day on, the princess never smiled! Names were collected from all over the land. They tried all the usual names such as Jane, Catherine, Amanda. They tried more unusual names such as Araminta, Tallulah, Leanora. They even tried quite outlandish names such as Dorominty, Truditta, Charlottamina. But none broke the spell.

Princess Columbine grew up to be a sweet and beautiful girl. Everybody loved her. But her face was always so sad, it made the king and queen unhappy. They tried everything to make her smile. They bought her a puppy. They even hired a court jester who told the silliest jokes you've ever heard.

"Why did the pecans cross the road?"asked the jolly jester. The princess shrugged.

"Because they were nuts!" the jester laughed.

"Why did the ice-cream?" the jester tried again. The princess just gazed politely.

"Because the jelly wobbled!"

One day an artist called Rudolpho came to the palace and asked the king if he could paint the princess's portrait. The king agreed on one condition.

He had to paint the princess smiling. Rudolpho set up his easel beneath a large mirror and began straight away. The princess sat opposite watching him paint in the mirror behind him. As he worked, Rudolpho asked the princess about all the people in the palace. He had soon painted the princess's portrait, all except for her smile. But he couldn't make the princess smile.

Rudolpho tried some funny drawings. He drew silly pictures of the king and queen. The princess looked on politely. Then he drew a picture of her old nurse and gave her a moustache, and above he wrote NURSE. Princess Columbine gazed in the mirror. There, above the picture, was the word NURSE spelled out back to front – ƎƧЯUИ.

“ESRUN,” Princess Columbine said quietly. And then she smiled. “Her name is ESRUN!” laughed Princess Columbine. At last the spell was broken! The king and queen heard her laughter and came rushing to see what was happening. They were so happy that soon everyone in the palace was laughing too.

The Tale of Two PRINCESSES

Long ago there were twin princesses called Charmina and Charlotte. Even though they were twins, the princesses were very different. In fact they were opposites. Princess Charmina was gracious and charming to everyone. She curtsied politely to the king and queen. And she stood quite still while the royal dressmakers came to fit her new ball gown.

Princess Charlotte was very different!

"Why do I have to dress like a puffball?" grumbled Princess Charlotte when it was her turn to have a new ball gown fitted.

"How dare you speak to us like that!" her parents cried.

But she did dare. She dared to run barefoot through the gardens until her hair looked like a bush. She dared to wear her shabbiest clothes. In fact, she didn't behave like a princess at all!

One day there was to be a ball at the palace. The guests of honour were two princes from the next kingdom. The two princesses, dressed in their new ball gowns, kept getting in the way of the preparations. "Why don't you go for a walk until our guests arrive?" suggested the queen. "But stay together, don't get dirty and don't be late!"

The two princesses walked to the bottom of the palace gardens.

"Let's go into the forest," said Princess Charlotte to her sister.

"I don't think we should," said Princess Charmina. "Our gowns will get dirty." But Princess Charlotte had already set off.

"Wait for me!" called Princess Charmina. "We must stay together!" They wandered deeper and deeper into the forest. They crunched through fallen leaves, listening to the birds singing.

"I think we should go back," Princess Charmina told her sister. "We'll be late for the ball."

Just then they heard a strange noise.

"Let's turn back!" said Princess Charmina, afraid.

"It may be someone in distress!" said Princess Charlotte. "We must go and help!"

Although Princess Charmina was scared, she agreed. "But we must get back in time for the ball."

"Don't worry, we will," said Princess Charlotte.

They set off again going even deeper into the forest. Finally, they came upon two horses in a clearing, but there was no sign of their riders. Just then they heard voices calling out,

"Who's there?"

At first, the two princesses couldn't see where the voices were coming from. In the middle of the clearing there was a large pit – an old bear trap. They peered over the edge. Princess Charmina clapped her hand over her mouth in astonishment. Princess Charlotte burst out laughing. There at the bottom of the pit were two princes.

"How do you do?" said the first prince.

"Well, don't just stand there," said the second prince. "Help us out!"

The two princesses found ropes and threw one end down to the princes. They tied the other end to their horses. Soon the princes were rescued and laughed with the princesses. They all set off to the palace together.

On their return they found everyone in the palace in a state of panic. The king and queen were angry when their daughters returned late looking so dirty. But their anger turned to joy when the two princes explained what had happened.

Everyone enjoyed the ball. The two princesses danced all night with the two princes. And, do you know, from that time on, Charlotte paid more attention to her gowns and hair. And Charmina became a little more playful and daring than before!

Written by Gaby Goldsack and
Jan and Tony Payne (Likely Stories)
Illustrated by Alison Atkins, Martin Grant (Advocate),
Daniel Howarth (Advocate), Paula Martyr, Peter Rutherford
and Rory Tyger (Advocate)
Language consultant: Betty Root
Design by Design Principals

This is a Parragon Book
This edition published 2002

Parragon
Queen Street House
4 Queen Street
Bath BA1 1HE, UK

Printed in China

ISBN (hardback) 0-75258-603-3
ISBN (paperback) 0-75258-604-1

The End